AEB1779

D1366128

COURTYARDS
&
PATIOS

COURTYARDS & PATIOS

Designing and Landscaping Elegant Outdoor Spaces

Discarded
By The
Six Mile Regional Library District

Chuck Crandall
and Barbara Crandall

01–4851

FRIEDMAN/FAIRFAX
PUBLISHERS

A FRIEDMAN/FAIRFAX BOOK
Friedman/Fairfax Publishers
15 West 26 Street
New York, NY 10010
Telephone (212) 685-6610
Fax (212) 685-1307
Please visit our website: www.metrobooks.com

© 2000, 1998 by Michael Friedman Publishing Group, Inc.

All rights reserved. No part of this publication may be reproduced,
stored in a retrieval system, or transmitted, in any form or by any
means, electronic, mechanical, photocopying, recording, or otherwise,
without prior written permission from the publisher.

Library of Congress Cataloging-in-Publication Data available upon request.

ISBN 1-58663-010-5

Editor: Susan Lauzau
Art Director: Jeff Batzli
Designers: Andrea Karman and Karen Philips
Photography Editor: Karen Barr
Production Manager: Camille Lee

Color separations by Radstock Reproductions
Printed in Hong Kong by Midas Printing Co. Ltd.

1 3 5 7 9 10 8 6 4 2

Distributed by Sterling Publishing Co., Inc.
387 Park Avenue South
New York, NY 10016-8810
Orders and customer service (800) 367-9692
Fax: (800) 542-7567
E-mail: custservice@sterlingpub.com
Website: www.sterlingpublishing.com

712.6
CRA

ACKNOWLEDGMENTS

We are deeply grateful to the wonderful homeowners, some of whom designed their own gardens or amenities, for sharing their private outdoor spaces with us. They include Gregg and Pam Bunch, Robert and Mary Lou Canady, Dick and Sue Coleman, The Cormier Family, The Dahl Family, Jim and Kaye Drennan, Dr. and Mrs. Nicholas Ellyn, Loren and Nandine Evinger, Susan Feller, Erik and Irina Gronborg, The Maron Family, Dick and Kate Maxey, The Miller-Johnson Family, Harold and Virginia Nelson, Dick and Geri Peterson, Captain Philip and Helen Rush, Harland and Martha Schroth, Donald and DeeDee Sodaro, David Steinberg, and Megan Timothy.

Additionally, we would like to recognize the talents of the many designers whose work appears in this book: Lani Berrington & Associates, Blue Sky Designs, Callaway Gardens, Robert C. Chesnut, ASLA, Environmental Creations, Inc./Michael Glassman, Charles E. Godfrey, Greg Grisamore & Associates, John Herbst, Jr. & Associates, ASLA, la STUDIO, Paradise Designs, Bo Powell, Architect, Rathfon Designs, Ivy Reid, Rogers Gardens, Jeff Stone Associates, Dennis Tromburg, Jim Whaley, and Nick Williams & Associates.

CONTENTS

CHAPTER ONE | GRAND ENTRANCES | 8

CHAPTER TWO | PATIOS WITH PERSONALITY | 22

CHAPTER THREE | PLANTS, PLANTERS &
PLANT POCKETS | 40

CHAPTER FOUR | CONTAINER GARDENS | 56

CHAPTER FIVE | ARBORS, TRELLISES &
OTHER STRUCTURES | 88

CHAPTER SIX | PRIVACY, SAFETY & SECURITY | 100

CHAPTER SEVEN | FOUNTAINS & WATER FEATURES | 116

CHAPTER EIGHT | DINING ALFRESCO | 128

PLANT HARDINESS ZONES | 140

SOURCES | 141

INDEX | 143

CHAPTER ONE

GRAND ENTRANCES

THE CLASSIC

COURTYARD

ONE OF THE MOST USEFUL AND

DESIRABLE FEATURES OF THE LAND-

SCAPE IS THE FRONT ENTRY COURTYARD,

A MODERN INTERPRETATION OF AN

ANCIENT CONVENTION.

Rivers of sensuous color invite visitors into this stunning courtyard,
drawing them ever closer to the house's entrance.

❖-❖-❖-❖

Private yet welcoming with its open gate, this courtyard promises more secrets to discover just around the corner.

Though the concept of a courtyard entry originated with the earliest civilizations in the Middle East, as surviving manuscripts and archeological relics illustrate, the courtyard's widespread use as a residential landscape feature is much more recent. Courtyards today provide both privacy and security—and they can also become multi-use spaces for the family. As space in cities and suburbs continues to be at a premium, more and more families look to the courtyard as a way to shelter themselves from public view and provide a greater measure of safety.

Foremost among the benefits of a courtyard is that it can expand living space by providing a new, outdoor room. Beyond serving merely as a transition from public street to private entry, the extra space a courtyard offers is a boon to home-owners whose lots are small or whose homes are located in a congested neighborhood where outside space is limited and privacy is virtually nonexistent.

Many families have reclaimed some of the front yard for protected play space for the children. A fence or wall equipped with a lockable gate provides a secure place for youngsters within view of the front rooms of the house. Other homeowners opt to use this newfound space for outdoor entertainment or as a sheltered environment for personal pursuits such as sunbathing, casual dining, and curling up with a book. Making the best use of the front yard becomes even more important when other outdoor facilities are limited or unavailable, as is the case in many twin home and town house developments.

Above left: A well-traveled street disappears behind an attractive wall screen in this Spanish-style courtyard. The fountain at the wall base helps mask the sound of traffic beyond. Above right: Whimsy sets the theme for this artists' courtyard gallery featuring ceramic plates and wall decorations by the noted ceramist Erik Gronborg.

MATCHING STYLES

While gaining privacy and security may be sufficient motivation for planning a courtyard entry, one of the best reasons for adding a courtyard is that you can create wonderful views from the front rooms of the house. Instead of settling for a view of traffic and neighbors' houses, you can create your own vision of beauty in the form of a garden room. You might even choose a garden theme that matches your interior design—a contemplative garden sets the mood for a Japanese-style interior, while a cottage-style planting acts as a preview for a casual country decor.

We know two couples, each with very different tastes, who extended the design of their interior into their new garden room when they decided to convert a portion of their front yard into a courtyard. One couple lives in the Southwest, where the wisest gar-

❖❖❖❖

Tucked between two houses, this lovely English-style courtyard garden manages to fit several charming features into a minuscule space.

dening choice is to work with nature and select native plants that flourish in this sometimes inhospitable climate. They chose their plants from a desert palette that included a palo verde tree (*Cercidium floridum*) and a selection of cacti and other succulents, some displayed in planters and pots. In addition, they arranged groupings of ollas and decorative terra-cotta pots, as well as interpretive sculptures of various Native American mythical figures. The steel sculptures were allowed to weather and rust naturally. This tableau set the scene for their home, which was filled with kachinas and Native American pottery. The other couple fashioned a formal

French garden in their courtyard, complete with parterres and sculptured junipers flanking the entry. Their interior features French country–style furniture and period antiques.

By using a little imagination, you can quite easily wed your garden to your house's interior. Take a look at your decor and borrow a few key elements for your courtyard garden design. If your style is casual and carefree, let your garden reflect that look with informal plantings and whimsical accents; if minimalism is more to your taste, plan your courtyard in the spare, pared-down style of a modern interior. You may even choose to tie your courtyard garden and interior together with a well-orchestrated color theme, in which a particular color or color combination dominates.

FLOORING FOR THE COURTYARD

A herringbone pattern of bricks combined with ribbons of a groundcover called dichondra make an interesting floor in this small-scale courtyard. Other matting groundcovers that work well in this situation are creeping thyme and pennyroyal.

Another, and much simpler, method of marrying indoor and outdoor spaces is with similar flooring materials. One of the most appealing paving solutions for outdoor rooms is to use the same flooring, where practical, that was used indoors. This not only creates a smooth visual transition from exterior to interior, but reinforces the impression that the garden room is an extension of the indoor space.

The major flooring options for interior and exterior use include flagstone, slate, granite, ceramic tile, and—more and more—tinted and sometimes textured concrete that has been sealed for better stain resistance.

This design option is not for everyone. Many homeowners still prefer a warmer, softer interior flooring such as wall-to-wall carpet-

❖◦❖◦❖◦❖

Cascading plants such as this Lady Banks' rose tumble over walls and fences, to create charming accents in the courtyard garden.

ing or wood. But especially in warm-climate regions, where indoor-outdoor living is often a year-round proposition, easy-care indoor-outdoor surfaces are finding favor among a growing number of families, particularly those with lots of children and pets who can inflict damage of biblical proportions on interior (and exterior!) floors.

A description of the many choices of flooring materials and a comparison of their relative merits are covered in detail in the following chapter. The favorite paver in North America is the clay brick in its many earthy hues, set either in sand or mortar. Because of the labor-intensive nature of laying a brick floor, this is among the most

expensive choices, though it is not as costly as some of the quarried stones such as granite, whose shipping and per-square-foot costs are significantly higher. Brick works well with nearly all architectural and garden styles and has a nostalgic warmth that many people like.

From a safety standpoint, the flooring in an entry courtyard must be smooth and even, and must provide good traction in wet weather, since it is a space open to guests and well traveled by the family. Patios, which are seldom used in poor weather, can be a bit rougher underfoot. For example, stones with somewhat uneven surfaces may be used, or matting groundcovers may be planted between pavers.

✦✦✦✦

Above left: Walls that surround courtyards and patios need to be a bit over 6 feet (1.8m) to maintain privacy. Here the large expanse of wall is softened by cool fingers of ivy. Above right: High walls, dressed with greenery to soften their mass, provide a private family space and an elegant garden courtyard.

ENCLOSING THE COURTYARD

There are three options for permanent enclosures for the courtyard or patio—hedges, fences, and walls. (These options are described in detail in chapter 6.) Fences are relatively inexpensive; they go up fast and offer long and dutiful service. Designed and stained or painted to harmonize with the house, fences may also offer a much-needed structural element to the garden. Walls evoke feelings of permanance and solidity and are by far the most expensive to erect,

*Effective yet friendly, this hedge of
English laurel (Prunus laurocerasus)
shields this courtyard facing a busy street
and helps buffer traffic noise.*

owing to the cost of materials and the many hours of handcraftsmanship required. But unlike hedges or fences, which require varying degrees of upkeep, walls are easy to maintain.

In addition to their more practical functions of providing security and privacy and blocking unappealing views beyond your property, fences and walls have aesthetic value: first, merely because of their appearance; second, because they provide a scaffold for climbing plants and a neutral foil for shrubs grown against them. Dazzling effects can be accomplished by training espaliers of fruiting and flowering species against walls and fences or by coaxing climbers such as Lady Banks' rose (*Rosa banksiae*) and honeysuckle (*Lonicera* spp.) over them.

Hedging

Hedges are the "friendliest" of all barriers, and are also the least expensive. If you feel you don't need a wall or fence around your courtyard but you want to install something to enclose and define the space, hedging is the answer. For hundreds of years, hedges have served as living fences and continue to be used in England and throughout the Continent. Unlike fences or walls, hedges are not instant solutions, as they require several years to fill in.

There are two types of hedges—formal and informal. Formal hedges are sheared and shaped, so you must have access to them on both sides. Some of the shrubs chosen for formal hedges include boxwood (*Buxus* spp.), privet (*Ligustrum* spp.), and yew (*Taxus* spp.).

Above left: Screens and fencing with an Oriental theme blend harmoniously into this serene garden. Above right: With minimal space between houses in many cities and suburban developments, screens, fences, and walls are the most expedient way to gain privacy. Well-designed enclosures, such as this one, help set the theme for a garden room.

Informal hedges are allowed to develop on their own, usually with only light clippings to head them back to the desired height. Flowering species are often chosen since their blooms won't be sheared off, as with formal hedges. Some popular choices include glossy abelia (*Abelia* × *grandiflora*), escallonia (*Escallonia rubra*), rhododendrons (*Rhododendron* spp.), and roses (*Rosa* spp.).

When choosing shrubs and trees, you also need to think about privacy and security if these are concerns. Since most city zoning regulations limit permanent barriers to 6 feet (1.8m) in height, you'll most likely have to add height with plants if you want a taller barrier. (For lists of specific plants for hedging see pages 103-104).

Screens

A number of evergreen and deciduous shrubs and trees have the mature height and breadth to serve as effective screens for outdoor rooms. When choosing such plants, analyze the characteristics of each and how it will help you achieve your goal. If, for example,

Above left: A combination of fencing and plantings helps shield this exposed patio from neighbors' view. As shrubs mature, screening will be even more effective. Above right: Nursery catalogs are full of helpful hints on selecting, planting, and caring for new introductions and old favorites, and many also contain charts of floral colors and plant height and girth.

you want year-round screening, opt for an evergreen type. If screening in the winter is not an important consideration, a deciduous species will serve.

If a wall encloses the courtyard, one way to achieve more height is to install troughs along the wall's top and plant dwarf evergreen shrubs that will provide another 2 to 3 feet (60 to 90cm) of screening. Another, more conventional solution is to install privacy plantings of tall-growing species on the courtyard side of the wall. Courtyards generally receive ample sunlight, so choices of trees and shrubs are limited only by regional considerations.

To deter prowlers, shrubs with thorns or spiny foliage are good choices planted against the enclosing fence or wall, although this option may not be suitable if small children will be using the courtyard for their play site. Some thorny species appropriate for this purpose include Korean barberry (*Berberis koreana*), Japanese barberry (*Berberis thunbergii*), natal plum (*Carissa macrocarpa*, Zones 9–10), silverberry (*Elaeagnus pungens*—there are also gold- and silver-edged variegated forms), holly (*Ilex* spp.), firethorn (*Pyracantha* spp.), rose (*Rosa* spp.), and yew (*Taxus* spp.—note that English yew *[T. baccata]* produces red berries with poisonous seeds).

PLANNING COURTYARD AND PATIO GARDENS

Because courtyards and patios feature so many hardscape elements concentrated in a small area, they usually need the softening effect of plants to make them more inviting. A large expanse of paving assailed by hot summer sun is not a pleasant place to spend much time. A few medium-growth trees and shrubs will moderate the effects of the sun and provide some welcome shade.

Even though a professional may be preparing the construction drawings and installing your courtyard or patio garden, you should involve yourself in the planning stage to ensure that what you end up with is what you want. The most expedient method of accomplishing this is to make a detailed drawing illustrating what you have in mind and to share it with your design consultant.

On graph paper, record the outline of your house using a scale of ⅛" = 1' (3mm = 30cm). Next, sketch the proposed courtyard or patio area, making sure to include walls, fences, planters, and other special features on your plan. Use your imagination to allocate various zones for activities such as barbecuing, reading, or dining.

Small gardens aren't difficult to create. Your primary considerations should be exposure and scale. The direction your garden faces often has a bearing on what plants will prosper there—some species have definite preferences for either sun or shade, while others like a combination of both. In addition, you should choose trees and shrubs with an eye toward mature height and girth. A tree that dwarfs the garden or that outgrows its space is a vexing problem. Consult chapter 3 for lists of medium-growth shrubs and trees for your garden.

As you plan your garden, whether you intend to plant it yourself or hire a professional to design and install it, there are a few basics to keep in mind:

• Most flowering and fruiting species, like the majority of vegetables, need at least 4 to 6 hours of direct sunlight each day to bloom and bear.

• Deciduous broad-leaf trees and shrubs will litter yards and patios with fallen leaves. Those trees and shrubs that also produce

Above left: Vibrant blue flooring and awning make this entrance stand out. Matching chairs and potted plants create a welcoming atmosphere. Above right: Special flooring treatments, such as these river rocks embedded in mortar and surrounded by bricks, add visual interest to courtyards and patios.

blooms, catkins, seeds, and berries are the messiest of all. Fallen fruit can stain hardscape surfaces, especially material like flagstone. Even so, an area that faces south or west may need the summer shade provided by a honey locust (*Gleditsia triacanthos*) or maple (*Acer* spp.) despite the autumn cleanup they require.

• In spaces where people congregate and children play, it's a good idea to eliminate from your plant list any species that are poisonous, produce thorns, or attract lots of bees, such as firethorn (*Pyracantha* spp.), Japanese barberry (*Berberis thunbergii*), and holly (*Ilex* spp.).

SPECIAL FEATURES FOR
COURTYARDS

Since courtyards are really front entry patios, they can be furnished with many of the same features that grace traditional patios. In fact, homeowners who have no other outdoor space of any consequence

Above left: Although the courtyard faces a city street, carefully placed trees and shrubs provide this family with privacy for their outdoor breakfasts.
Above right: This spacious courtyard, with its several seating areas, is a stellar example of an outdoor area designed for family use and entertainment.
The raised planters are constructed to provide additional seating at a comfortable height.

use their courtyard for alfresco dining, as an overflow entertainment area, or as a safe containment area for children and pets—in short, the courtyard becomes a site for all at-home outdoor activities.

This range of uses may mean that the courtyard is outfitted with dining furniture and other seating, play equipment, treillage arches and shade umbrellas, fountains, water gardens, and other decorative embellishments.

If there are side yards on your property, there should be access to them from the courtyard. This eliminates the awkwardness of having to haul garden tools and—if the space is also used as a play area—toys and other paraphernalia through the house. In cases where outdoor spaces such as a backyard and side yards are available for the family's use, the courtyard can be devoted primarily to serving as an elegant reception vestibule for guests and as a stunning cloistered garden.

❖ ❖ ❖ ❖

Patios are more private spaces. Remote from view, they are areas where family members can enjoy the outdoors in a more relaxed mood. These relatively secluded retreats are explored in the next chapter.

CHAPTER TWO

PATIOS WITH PERSONALITY

Each house has its own distinct character, and the family that resides in it has its own special needs and desires when it comes to outdoor relaxation and recreation. For these reasons, a preliminary patio design, no matter how basic, should be prepared by those who will use it.

This gardener conquered a steep slope to reclaim space for a virtual oasis. Informal dining is clearly one of this family's favorite pastimes.

As with the design of a courtyard, be sure to involve yourself in every step of the planning, even if you plan to hire a professional to refine and execute the plan. Make a detailed drawing on graph paper, including the outline and dimensions of your house and noting the permanent features that may be affected or damaged by construction. These include underground electrical conduits and gas or sewer lines. Several years ago we overlooked this detail during a patio installation. As a result of this oversight we contributed handsomely to our plumber's vacation fund when a contractor's backhoe fractured the waste pipe running to the septic tank.

After you've finished the outline of the features that exist on your property, sketch the proposed patio area onto the plan. Use a scale of ⅛" = 1' (3mm = 30cm) to lay out the patio configuration; this will allow you to compare space allocations for each feature and decide

Rather than pour one massive slab, the designer of this attractive patio chose to break up the hard surfaces into freeform "islands" surrounded by turf grass. The concrete has been tinted to blend with the house.

if something appears out of scale. Using tracing paper overlays or several photocopies of the plan, indicate where you want to put walls, fences, planters, barbecue pits, built-in benches, sandboxes, and other special features.

DETERMINING SIZE AND SHAPE

As a first step you should decide on the size and shape of the patio. There are some designers who believe that a patio should be no larger than the biggest room in the house, but this rule can be somewhat limiting. Instead, let the size of your patio be governed by the amount of space needed to comfortably fit all the features you want.

A large patio can always be broken up visually by "zoning" it for various activities. This can be easily accomplished with changes in level, low walls or planters that divide the space, built-in benches, a

Above left: A spacious patio features handsome stone steps leading down into the yard. This is a great way to landscape a sloped area between house and yard. Above right: Patios don't have to be rectilinear; any shape that fits the site may be used. This area off the master bedroom is best served with a rounded patio.

roofed dining or cookout area, changes in flooring materials, or even strategically placed potted trees. Use your imagination to develop defined areas for specific activities.

Special areas can also be delineated by the shape of the patio. A peninsula extending off the main area, for example, can provide a sunbathing nook or a children's play area. Patios are generally rectangular or square, but they can be any shape you want, including circular or semicircular. Straight edges maximize the available space, but if space conservation is not important, the curving lines of an arc are more pleasing to the eye.

ANALYZING THE SITE

The type of exposure you have will often dictate how a patio is used and what plant material can be grown on and around it. Sites that face south or west will be brightest and will get the most sun during summer months. This means that patios with either southern or western exposure are ideal for ornamental gardens, roses and other flowering shrubs, herbs, and berry bushes and fruit trees. This type of exposure is also ideal for sunbathing. The intensity of the sun's rays can be moderated in sections by constructing arbors, pergolas, or roof structures. Sheltering trees planted on the perimeter of the patio will filter sunlight through their leafy canopies.

Western exposures are the hottest and, without the addition of some screening, are often too bright for comfort as the sun begins its descent. A grove of trees or a garden structure such as a pergola is usually needed to make west-facing patios tolerable in the late afternoon.

North-facing spaces are the shadiest and, consequently, the coolest during the torrid summer months. They offer a good location for a reading nook or a restful retreat. Shade-loving plants in a north-facing spot will add to the illusion of a secluded forest glen.

To create harmony of design, the same flagstone was used here for flooring, planters, and cookout station. Curved lines provide another eye-pleasing ingredient.

A wide choice of natural and manufactured materials is available in a variety of colors and textures. Most surface options have both pluses and minuses. Following are the most important things to consider when choosing a paving material.

Surface Characteristics

As a rule, fairly smooth, flat surfaces are the easiest to navigate, but some materials, such as glazed tiles or smooth-finished concrete, may be treacherous when wet. In damp climates brick may become coated with a patina of moss, which can also be slippery underfoot.

EVALUATING PAVING OPTIONS

Patio floors should be chosen with beauty and durability in mind, and ideally should be tailored to meld harmoniously with the house.

If you love the look of tiles, don't despair; there are nonskid glazed tiles designed for exterior use. Concrete, too, can be given a number of different treatments that will make its surface safe to walk on in wet weather (see page 31). Moss that develops on brick

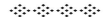

Brick is one of the most popular materials for building patios and other hardscape elements in the home landscape. It has a warmth and adaptability that blends with most architectural styles.

in damp, shaded environments can be removed by scrubbing surfaces periodically with a stiff broom or brush.

Surfaces that contain raised stones or irregular exposed edges, such as fieldstone or flagstone, may pose an equal risk for tripping and falling, especially for the elderly and for rambunctious children. When choosing a flooring material, make sure to avoid uneven surfaces, no matter how beautiful they might look.

Appropriateness and Appearance

Many homeowners are concerned with selecting the paving material that best complements the architectural style of their home. Brick, flagstone, bluestone, and other kinds of paving stone are all appropriate choices for traditional home styles—Victorian, Colonial, ranch, and cottage. For contemporary architecture, ceramic tile (in mild-winter climates), stamped or tinted concrete, or concrete pavers may be more apropos. Of all the paving materials, brick is the universal favorite for patio and courtyard floors, but it may seen too old-fashioned when juxtaposed with a sleek, modern house.

Brick

For thousands of years, bricks made of sun-dried or fired clay have been used for paving. Today, brick is still the most popular choice for building attractive, long-lasting patios, walks, and walls. Clay brick has a warmth and visual appeal unequaled by any other mate-

The beauty and appeal of brick for patio flooring can be seen in this large patio, which features the popular herringbone pattern.

rial. Even after generations of harsh weather, foot traffic, and abuse, brick maintains its character and integrity.

But is brick an appropriate hardscape material for all house styles? Purists would say no, that much contemporary architecture requires something a bit colder, such as concrete. For all but the most modern residences, though, brick is probably the ideal choice for paving large expanses without overpowering the eye. A possible exception might be used brick, either salvaged from demolition sites or manufactured; used brick tends to have a "busy" look when concentrated in a small space because of its chalky patina and concrete residue.

Color has a lot to do with the appeal brick holds for most people. It is available in a surprising range of hues, from oranges and reds to ochers and browns. Tints are produced both by the chemical composition of the clay and by the method and temperature used in the firing process.

For patio construction, common or paving brick is usually chosen because of its reasonable price. There are three types of common brick: clinker, which is rough-surfaced with flashed patches; sand mold, which has rounded edges and a smooth surface; and wire cut, which has a rough and pitted surface and sharp edges.

Brick is rated for three exposures: SW, severe weathering, which means it is suitable for even the harshest climates; MW, medium weathering, appropriate for use in subfreezing but not subzero temperatures; and NW, no weathering, an interior brick. Only the first two are acceptable for patio construction.

Bricks can also be used to construct integrated planters and walls around masonry patios or courtyards, but there is a danger of creating too much "mass" in small patio spaces. Judgments of this kind are where the experienced eye of a professional designer is useful.

Compared with concrete, brick is more expensive, especially the popular used bricks and face bricks (the costliest), which are used to

❖❖❖❖❖

Concrete is unsurpassed as a flooring material, and when given a tint or special finish such as the embedded aggregate shown above, it takes on a special character.

veneer buildings and walls. The cost can be reduced if splits—bricks half as thick as standards—are used. These must be set in mortar on an existing concrete slab.

Concrete

To many homeowners, the mention of a concrete patio conjures up an image of a drab, utilitarian block that reflects an uncomfortable glare. But great strides have been made in recent years in perfecting finishing techniques that can transform a newly poured concrete patio into handsome, expensive-looking hardscape.

Existing concrete patios, too, can benefit from an array of refurbishing techniques. A plain concrete slab can be acid-washed and tinted by expert licensed contractors to give it an attractive finish, or it can be resurfaced with a veneer of colored or stamped concrete.

If a concrete patio is in good condition, it can also be used as a foundation for laying tiles, bricks, or other pavers in mortar if you wish to upgrade to another surface material without removing the existing patio.

TINTED FINISHES

Coloring concrete is a growing trend; new pigments produce gorgeous subtle colors. The ideal method of tinting concrete is adding

Above left: Elegant steps lead from the street to a sunken courtyard in this lovely landscape. Note that the central walk is actually a bridge that traverses a koi pond. Above right: This closeup of aggregate paving clearly shows the pebbles that are either added during the mixing or "salted" onto the surface and floated into freshly poured concrete.

color solutions while the material is being mixed. This ensures thorough saturation of the tint throughout the mix. Dry pigments may also be sprinkled over freshly floated concrete and mixed into the surface with a hand float. This technique calls for experience and may not always produce a consistent tint.

To change existing gray concrete to a colored surface, metallic salts and acid solutions are applied and allowed to stand for a while before being rinsed off. The result is a muted or slightly mottled tint that gives the surface a more appealing, organic look.

STAMPED FINISHES

Stamping and other mechanical techniques can simulate the look of brick or stone in an endless variety of shapes and textures. Stamping with various devices that resemble large cookie cutters has become the primary method of creating hardscape that closely resembles flagstone, tile, brick, and other desirable paving material.

EXPOSED AGGREGATE FINISHES

An exposed aggregate finish is another popular choice for a new concrete patio. Small, smooth gravel, river rock, or pebbles are gen-

❖·❖·❖·❖

Masquerading as a terra-cotta tiled patio, the surface here is actually tinted, scored, and sealed concrete that will maintain its good looks for the life of the patio. The warm tint of the concrete sets off the cool greens of plants and the sparkling water.

erally added to the concrete as it is being mixed, or the gravel may be "salted" over the surface of a freshly poured slab and pressed into the surface with a float.

ROCK SALT FINISHES

A rock salt finish is used to give concrete a pitted surface that reduces its slipperiness in wet weather. The salt is spread over the damp concrete by hand, then pressed lightly into the surface with a float. After the slab has cured for a few days, the undissolved salt is hosed off.

BROOM AND SEMISMOOTH FINISHES

Another technique for creating surfaces with good wet-weather traction is to make minute grooves in damp concrete with a clean, new push broom. This is done by drawing the broom lightly across the slab with either straight or waved strokes. A similar effect can

A handsome and durable courtyard floor has been created with dressed Pennsylvania blue stone, a popular paving material in the East.

also be achieved by using a wood float; this creates what is known as a semismooth finish.

CONCRETE PAVERS

Pressure-formed concrete pavers—from hexagonal to octagonal to circular to square—come in a dazzling array of colors, shapes, sizes, thicknesses, and textures. These versatile pavers are tough and inexpensive when compared with the cost of most other materials.

Some people think concrete pavers look too "commercial" and lack the character and warmth of more familiar pavers, such as brick and stone. While it is true that many of the durable interlocking styles are being installed in commercial and municipal projects such as streets, sidewalks, and civic promenades, this should not preclude their use on residential patios and walks. Because they are made from very dense concrete in thicknesses from half an inch (12mm) to more than three inches (7.5cm), concrete pavers are suitable for patios and other hardscape applications, even in areas with very severe winters.

Cast concrete pavers, like these interlocking blocks, may be laid on a bed of sand or set in mortar to fashion an attractive, cost-effective patio floor.

PAINTING AND STAINING

Existing concrete surfaces that are in good condition may be painted or stained. While painting is an option, it is one that should be carefully considered before it is done. Because both foot traffic and weather can wear away the paint, leaving a mottled, uneven surface, it is not a wholly satisfactory solution. Still, if paint is applied carefully and touched up periodically, it can be a quick, inexpensive method of covering a badly soiled surface. Before a concrete slab can be painted, it must cure for three to six months, then be power-washed to remove dirt and any leached chemical residue. Once the surface is thoroughly dry, a primer and paint formulated for coating concrete may be used, allowing twenty-four hours of drying time between applications.

❖❖❖ ❖❖ ❖❖ ❖❖❖

A large patio has been "zoned" into more intimate spaces with planting beds, containers, and accessories. The flooring is flagstone set in mortar.

Because of its lack of durability, tough stains that stand up well to traffic and weather are usually a better choice. Concrete stains, like paints, are applied with a roller but they do a better job of penetrating concrete than paints do. Before concrete can be successfully stained, its pH level must be neutralized by acid etching using a mixture of two parts water to one part muriatic acid. If you are planning this project, be sure to wear old clothing, eye protection, and rubber gloves. You can find concrete stains in most large home improvement centers and building supply stores.

Stone

Natural stone is the oldest building material, and its popularity remains undiminished after thousands of years. For patio, terrace, and courtyard flooring, stone will outlast brick or concrete and provide a durable and beautiful surface unaffected by weather, foot traffic, or the passage of time.

Before you choose a stone, it helps to know a bit about the geology of the earth and how each of the three classifications of stone was formed. Igneous rock includes adoquin, basalt, bluestone, granite, and marble. These volcanic rocks yield the hardest, most durable surfaces. Metamorphic rock, including Idaho quartzite and slate, has been changed in composition under tremendous geothermal heat, pressure, and chemical action, which can transform limestone into marble and granite into gneiss, a banded stone with alternating layers of feldspar, hornblende, mica, and quartz. Sedimentary rock, of which limestone and sandstone are the most common examples, is created from sedi-

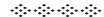

Almost universally available, fieldstone is a popular, virtually indestructible paving material unaffected by even severe weather. Here, dressed stone is laid with groundcover grouting.

ments that have been compressed under incredible pressure during the formation of the earth.

Stone is unequaled in beauty and permanence, but it has a downside—the price. Because of its weight, shipping costs can make it prohibitively expensive—three or four times what concrete or brick would be, in some instances. Locally quarried stone, however, is comparable in price to brick and concrete because of the considerable savings on freight charges.

FIELDSTONE

As the name implies, fieldstone is plentiful in meadows and fields, and has been the bane of many a farmer whose plow blades have been dulled and dented by it. It has a broad range of color and texture, evident in the many walls constructed with it throughout the world.

Most fieldstones used as paving are cut or dressed into shapes that make them suitable for patios or walks. They can be used to create colorful and handsome hardscape flooring or, on a smaller scale, to add an accent to a patio constructed of other material.

FLAGSTONE

This attractive stone forms either as flat plates in the earth or in massive deposits of rock that split neatly into layers of varying thickness. Colors generally range from a light, sometimes pinkish, tan (Arizona flag) to a dull charcoal gray (Bouquet Canyon stone). Probably the most common of the flags are limestone and sandstone.

Typically, flagstones are 1 to 2 inches (2.5 to 5cm) thick, although some may be thinner or thicker, depending upon the source. Some quarries cut the stone into "tiles" that can be laid in builder's sand or mortar. As a rule, though, part of the appeal of flag and other

undressed stone is the patterns that can be created by carefully fitting the irregular shapes into a harmonious design.

Flagstones—especially sandstone and limestone—do have an Achilles' heel. Because of their inherent porousness, they can absorb water. In areas of subzero winter temperatures, the trapped moisture can freeze, and the cycle of freezing and thawing that can heave plants out of the soil can also fracture flagstone. For this reason, if you live in a severe-winter region, an igneous stone might be a better paving choice.

The absorptive character of flagstone also means that it is subject to staining from oily liquid spills. If this poses an aesthetic problem for you, flag is probably not the stone to use around dining and cookout areas.

DRESSED STONE

Many larger landscape and building supply outlets stock a wide array of stone pavers and tiles that have been cut in modular dimensions. Some types that are commonly available in most geographic areas are flagstone, marble, quartzite, and slate, although regional stones may also be carried locally—such as adoquin and Arizona flag in the North American West and bluestone and granite in the East.

Opposite: A combination of Spanish pavers and tinted concrete helps create a Mediterranean mood when combined with the fabulous tiles and colorful plantings in this California landscape. Above: A favorite in the West and Southwest, Mexican pavers blend well with the Spanish architecture prevalent in these regions. Sealing is vital to prolonging the life of clay tiles, which can deteriorate when left untreated.

Ceramic Tile

Tile for exterior hardscaping is primarily used in mild climates that don't experience frosts and freezes, which can cause tile to fracture. Adobe is the exception, but shipping costs make it impractical outside the Southwest. For outdoors, unglazed tiles are the most sensible choice. Glazed tiles—even those with rough surfaces—can become dangerously slick when wet, though they can be used in ribbons on patio floors and for accents on stair risers.

A handsome patio of terra-cotta pavers is given a softening look when flanked with planting beds. The rose-colored pavers beautifully complement the sparkling waters of the pool.

There are four types of unglazed tile, all of which are molded and kiln-fired using varying temperatures and techniques to give them their unique characteristics and strength: pavers, which are available in the widest variety of sizes and materials, including terra-cotta; quarry tile, which comes in a number of earth tones; synthetic stone tile, manufactured to resemble granite, marble, sandstone, and slate in tints of tan, charcoal, and black; and adobe, a popular classic in the Southwest and southern California. Adobe, traditionally made of sun-dried earth, has been made into a durable paving material by the addition of an asphalt stabilizer, which doesn't affect the color but strengthens the tile and makes it resistant to the destructive effects of moisture and heat.

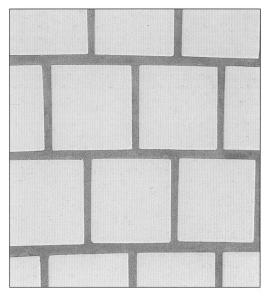

Above left: Clay pavers accent the Spanish styling of this home. Pavers made of clay are most durable in mild-winter climates, where they are unlikely to be damaged by repeated freezing and thawing. Above right: Glazed ceramic clay tile is another mild-climate favorite, but can become slippery in wet weather. For this reason, it is generally used as decorative trim rather than for the entire surface.

To protect terra-cotta tiles from the ravages of the weather and from permanent staining, they should be sealed with a penetrating sealer after installation, if they were not sealed at the factory. Because sealing tends to darken clay and give it a faint sheen, the sealer to be used should be tested on a tile to be certain the effect is not objectionable.

Ceramic tiles ¼ inch (6mm) thick are too thin to be set in a sand bed. They are made to be laid in mortar on a slab with grout between them to hold them in place. Tiles and pavers ½ inch to ¾ inch (12 to 20mm) thick may be installed in all the traditional ways: on a 1-inch (2.5cm) -deep sand bed, on compacted and level soil, with dry mortar, or in wet mortar. They may be grouted with sand, soil, or conventional grout tinted to match the tile's color or to contrast with it.

We've explored some things to think about as you plan your outdoor rooms—the ways you will use them and the hardscape materials you can choose to give you the best service. The next chapter introduces you to the many wonderful plant choices available for small-space gardens and shows you how to use them with style.

CHAPTER THREE

PLANTS, PLANTERS & PLANT POCKETS

IN MOST CASES, PATIOS AND COURTYARDS

CAN BE DESIGNED WITH BUILT-IN PLANTERS

AND WELLS THAT ARE IDEAL FOR GROWING

VIRTUALLY ANY SHRUB OR TREE THAT IS

ACCLIMATED TO THE REGION.

This handsome planter with seating-height walls
provides a shady haven on hot summer days.

❖❖❖❖❖

Planting beds with seating areas for viewing the seasonal show dominate this cheery patio.

The main difference between a courtyard or patio landscape and a traditional one is that paving substitutes for a lawn.

TYPES OF PLANTERS

In recent years landscape designers have favored planters incorporated into walls at convenient locations, such as along the base or flanking an entry. To blend integrated planters with their surroundings, it's desirable to choose the same materials that were used to build the house, fence, or wall—you might opt for stone, brick, wood, or concrete blocks dressed with a veneer of stone, half-bricks, or stucco.

If planters are open on the bottom to the native soil, plant roots can roam freely and the result will be shrubs and trees that reach their maximum size. But if the planters have bottoms like traditional containers, the roots may be somewhat confined. This often has a dwarfing effect on larger plants like shrubs and standards, and the result is smaller, but no less healthy, specimens. It is critical that these fully enclosed planters have holes near the base to let excess water drain; otherwise, the plant material will succumb to rot.

A novel approach to creating planter space in walls is to build troughs and pockets into the walls as they are being constructed. These innovative planters can even be constructed on top of the wall. Drainage pipes installed beneath the planters carry excess water down inside the wall, where it is channeled through vertical sections of PVC (polyvinyl chloride) pipe that can be inserted in the footing when it is poured.

On fences, planters made of the same wood may be attached to the fence or extended out from its base to form raised planters. It is especially harmonious when fence and planter are stained or painted

Planters built when walls are constructed and flooring laid are visually tied into the overall design. These planters are open to the native soil for drainage and have built-in irrigation lines.

so that they appear as one unit. Plants grown in these integrated planters soften the effect of the barrier and add colorful vertical interest in courtyards, patios, and narrow side yards.

Planters set into walls and attached to fences may be affixed at a height that makes it easier and more comfortable to garden, because much of the bending can be eliminated. Another plus—they add a touch of greenery at an unexpected level. It's also a nice idea to incorporate planters at seating height (20 to 22 inches [51 to 56cm]) alongside benches set into walls. The beauty and fragrance of the plants will make the benches an ever-popular spot.

PLANTS FOR SUNNY SITES

Most perennials, annuals, shrubs, and trees are acclimated to a full-sun exposure, although many perform quite nicely in a location that is shady for part of the day. Among these are a number of species native to the dry regions of South Africa, Australia, New Zealand, California, and the American Southwest. Consequently, not all of the following may be hardy in areas that experience sub-zero winters.

For Sunny Exposures
Achillea filipendulina (yarrow)
Anthemis punctata (chamomile)
Artemisia absinthium (common wormwood)
Aster novi-belgii 'Jenny' (Michaelmas daisy)
Berberis spp. (in variety) (barberry)
Buddleia alternifolia (butterfly bush)
Campanula persicifolia (peach-leaved bellflower)
Centaurea cyanus (bachelor's button)
Clarkia elegans (clarkia)
Convolvulus cneorum (bush morning glory)
Cotoneaster horizontalis (rock cotoneaster)

Cytisus × *kewensis* (broom)
Dianthus spp. (in variety) (pink)
Geranium spp. (in variety) (cranesbill)
Gypsophila paniculata (baby's breath)
Helianthemum 'Amy Baring' (rockrose)
Hypericum 'Hidcote' (Saint-John's-wort)
Kniphofia 'Royal Standard' (red-hot poker)
Lavandula angustifolia (lavender)
Liriope muscari (lilyturf)
Lychnis chalcedonica (Maltese cross)
Nepeta × *faassenii* (catmint)
Papaver orientale (oriental poppy)
Perovskia atriplicifolia (Russian sage)
Phlox paniculata (summer phlox)
Potentilla fruticosa (shrubby potentilla)
Rosmarinus officinalis (rosemary)
Stachys byzantina (lamb's ears)
Viola spp. (in variety) (viola, pansy)
Yucca filamentosa (Adam's needle)

Achillea filipendulina

Lavandula angustifolia

PLANT POCKETS AND WELLS

When courtyard and patio floors are poured or laid, you might wish to include spaces of various sizes and shapes that are open to the ground. These plant wells easily accommodate shrubs, trees, and bedding plants; because they are planted in ground soil, these plants will need less water and will overwinter more reliably. When filled with color and greenery, these niches soften the mass of hardscape that is necessary to create a patio floor of adequate dimensions.

A number of design techniques can be used to enhance plant wells. On a concrete patio, brick and stone make handsome trims that dress up the perimeter of the well openings. By raising the edging slightly above

❖❖❖❖❖

These plant wells have been constructed of the same stone used for the flooring, providing continuity of design. Because the space is small, the flowers can be replanted often to create lovely seasonal displays.

grade, you'll provide a nice finishing touch and help prevent a misstep into the planting bed.

For safety's sake, plant wells in entry courtyards should be located away from the primary accessway—around the perimeter of the courtyard is one popular choice—and illuminated with walk lights at night.

If you want the convenience of automatic irrigation for planters and welled gardens, install the pipes intended to serve these areas when the floor is poured or laid. An irrigation system avoids the bother and mess of hauling out a hose each time plants need water. Also, an automatic system, controlled by a timer, irrigates at specific times—a practical advantage when you're away from home for extended periods.

PLANTS FOR SHADY NOOKS

Most plants, especially those that bloom, need a few hours of sun each day to prosper. But there are a number of others that do best in a shady niche, a location that receives filtered sun, or a spot that has a part sun–part shade exposure.

Also, there are plants (many woodland ferns, mosses, and some ivies) that need evenly moist soil as well as a shady spot. Still other plants (all cacti and most other succulents, some ornamental grasses, and perennials such as bear's-breeches) require a period of drought between drenchings.

Keep in mind that exposure recommendations are merely that—recommendations based on general gardening experience. We encourage you to experiment; if a particular plant isn't prospering in one exposure, move it to another.

Moist Shade

Aconitum spp. (in variety) (monkshood, wolfbane)
Adiantum pedatum (northern maidenhair fern)
Astilbe spp. (in variety) (false goat's beard)
Begonia spp. (rex hybrids)
Brunneria macrophylla (Siberian bugloss)
Camellia spp. (in variety) (camellia)
Campanula lactiflora (milky bellflower)
Carex elata 'Aurea' (Bowles' garden sedge)
Clethra arborea (lily-of-the-valley tree)
Cornus spp. (in variety) (dogwood)
Dicentra spectabilis 'Alba' (bleeding heart)
Dodecatheon pulchellum (shooting star)
Dryopteris filix-mas (male fern)
Epimedium grandiflorum (bishop's hat)

Astilbe spp.

Fuchsia spp. (lady's eardrop)
Gaultheria procumbens (creeping wintergreen)
Gentiana asclepiadea (willow gentian)
Hedera helix (English ivy)
Helleborus orientalis (Lenten rose)
Hosta fortunei (plantain lily)
Houttuynia cordata 'Chameleon'
    (chameleon creeper)
Hydrangea anomala petiolaris (climbing
    hydrangea)
Impatiens spp. (impatiens)
Kalmia latifolia (mountain laurel)
Leucothoe fontanesiana (drooping leucothoe)
Mahonia aquifolium (Oregon grape)
Meconopsis cambrica (Welsh poppy)
Mentha suavolens (apple mint)
Oxalis acetosella (wood sorrel)
Paeonia lactiflora hybrids (peony)
Paeonia mlokosewitschii (Caucasian peony)
Phyllostachys viridistriatus (bamboo)
Polygonatum × hybridum (Solomon's seal)
Polypodium glycyrrhiza (licorice fern)
Rhododendron spp. (in variety) (azalea,
    rhododendron)
Smilacina racemosa (false Solomon's seal)
Stewartia pseudocamellia (Japanese stewartia)
Thalictrum aquilegifolium 'Album' (meadow rue)
Tradescantia spp. (in variety) (spiderwort)
Trillium grandiflorum (wake robin)
Trollius europaeus (globe flower)

Trillium grandiflorum

Euonymus fortunei

Tropaeolum speciosum (Scottish flame flower)
Vinca minor (dwarf periwinkle)

Dry Shade
Alchemilla spp. (lady's mantle)
Aucuba japonica (Japanese aucuba)
Berberis spp. (barberry)
Bergenia spp. (in variety) (bergenia)
Cotoneaster horizontalis (rock cotoneaster)
Digitalis spp. (in variety) (foxglove)

Euonymus fortunei cultivars (wintercreeper)
Fatsia japonica (Japanese aralia)
Helleborus spp. (hellebore)
Hosta spp. and hybrids (plantain lily)
Lamium maculatum (dead nettle)
Osmanthus spp. (in variety) (osmanthus)
Pachysandra terminalis (Japanese spurge)
Pulmonaria saccharata (Bethlehem sage)
Skimmia japonica (Japanese skimmia)

THE GOOD EARTH

A successful garden begins by matching plants with the type of soil they need to prosper. Only inexperienced gardeners ignore this important requirement, usually with disappointing results. This is especially true of species that prefer acidic soil, such as rhododendrons and azaleas, camellias, mountain laurel (*Kalmia latifolia*), and andromeda (*Pieris* spp.). These plants draw the extra iron they need for nutrition from acidic soil. If they can't get this vital element in sufficient quantities, their leaves begin to yellow (a condition called chlorosis) and they die. Iron supplements can be applied to the soil around plants suffering from chlorosis, which usually restores their vigor and color, but it is always a better course to avoid the problem from the outset.

How can you determine how acidic or alkaline your native soil is? You can either have it analyzed by a soil testing lab for a modest fee, or—for a basic pH analysis—you can do a litmus test yourself using a simple kit available at most garden centers.

The pH scale runs from 1 to 14, with 7.0 representing a neutral reading. A reading below 7.0 indicates the soil is acidic; a reading above 7.0 indicates the sample is alkaline and contains considerable levels of lime. Soil that is too alkaline can be acidified by blending in ground peat, leaf mold, or well-rotted compost. To raise the alkaline level, add agricultural lime.

The goal should always be to provide a nutrient-rich, fertile soil that retains moisture yet drains well. This perfect medium is called loam, or gardener's gold. Composted and organically deodorized

Above left: Acid or alkaline? An inexpensive pH meter can tell you whether you need to add amendments to your garden soil to bring it into balance. A professional soil test is even more reliable. Above right: Raised beds constructed when patio walls and flooring are installed, such as this one made of dry-laid flagstone, provide easy-to-tend mini gardens close to the house.

steer manure, sand, and sawdust fortified with organic nitrogen are all good amendments that will improve the texture and drainage properties of garden soil. Heavy clay soil can be improved structurally with the addition of agricultural gypsum, stabilized redwood sawdust, ground fir bark, or compost.

If you have good, well-balanced soil in your plant wells and in the garden beds surrounding your courtyard or patio, you shouldn't need to add any fertilizers to get the maximum performance from your plants, although most makers of fertilizer would probably disagree. If you feel you must use fertilizer, choose an organic one that will eventually break down and add texture to your soil. Chemical fertilizers are harsh and often don't fully dissolve in the ground. This leads to a buildup of fertilizer salts that can "burn" plants; excessive use of these synthetics can make the soil barren and devoid of the micronutrients necessary for good plant growth. Evidence of fertilizer salt buildup appears as white crusting on the surface of garden soil.

Nearly all organic, or natural, fertilizers are slow-acting, so their effect may not be seen for several days (even weeks). But they do work their magic eventually and help restore vitality and fertility to the soil.

BED AND BORDER PLANTS

Perimeter beds and borders filled with healthy, colorful plants create beautiful frames for the paved floors of outdoor rooms. With courtyard and patio perimeter gardens, the same rules used in conventional gardening apply: position lower-growing plants in front, medium-growth stock in the center, and taller species, including shrubs and trees, in the background.

Keep in mind that color can create certain illusions. Visually, warm colors appear to "advance" and cool colors tend to "recede." To make a smaller courtyard or patio space seem larger, flowers and foliage in cool blues and purples should be planted closer to the foreground than those in warm or hot colors like yellow, orange, and red.

ORGANIC FERTILIZERS
FOR THE GARDEN

Nitrogen is essential for good leaf development and color, and promotes vigorous growth in ornamentals. Phosphorous also contributes to healthy growth and spurs the development and viability of seeds. Potash, or potassium, is a vital element in promoting color and flavor in vegetables and fruit, as well as helping plants develop strong stems and vigorous roots.

The following chart shows the organic fertilizers that will add either nitrogen, phosporus, or potash to your garden soil.

Nitrogen	*Phosphorous*	*Potash*
Alfalfa meal (medium)	Alfalfa meal	Kelp meal
Barnyard manures (low)	Barnyard manures	Sul Po Mag
Bat guano (high)	Bat guano	
Blood meal (high)	Bone meal	
Cottonseed meal (medium)	Rock phosphate	
Feather meal (high)		
Fish meal (high)		
Soybean meal (medium)		

Container gardens are another resource for enhancing the appearance and enjoyment of patios and courtyards. The following chapter explores the possibilities and techniques of fashioning colorful portable gardens.

PLANTS FOR FRAGRANCE

Aroma is one of nature's inventions to ensure the continuation of a plant species. Sweet-smelling flowers attract pollinating bees and other insects. Scented blooms and aromatic leaves are an important part of the garden experience. Establish a fragrant garden or just add a few plants that produce evocative perfume by incorporating some of the following flowers and foliage to your yard.

Fragrant Flowers

Abelia chinensis (Chinese abelia)
Boronia heterophylla (red boronia)
Boronia serrulata (boronia)
Brachycome iberidifolia (swan river daisy)
Brugmansia candida (angel's trumpet)
Buddleia alternifolia (fountain butterfly bush)
Carpentaria californica (bush anemone)
Cestrum nocturnum (night-blooming jasmine)
Cheiranthus cheiri (wallflower)
Chimonanthus praecox (wintersweet)
Choisya ternata (Mexican orange)
Citrus spp. (grapefruit, lemon, orange)

Buddleia alternifolia

Clematis dioscoreifolia (sweet autumn clematis)
Cytisus battandieri (broom)
Daphne mantensiana (Manten's daphne)
Daphne odora (winter daphne)
Deutzia scabra 'Plena' (fuzzy deutzia)
Dianthus caryophyllus (carnation)
Freesia hybrids (freesia)
Galtonia candicans (summer hyacinth)
Gardenia jasminoides (gardenia)
Heliotropium arborescens (heliotrope)
Hoya carnosa (wax plant)
Hyacinthus spp. (hyacinth)
Jasminum multipartitum (African jasmine)
Jasminum nitidum (angelwing jasmine)
Jasminum polyanthum (Chinese jasmine)
Jasminum sambac (Arabian jasmine)
Lathyrus odoratus (sweet pea)
Lavandula × intermedia (old English lavender)
Lilium candidum (madonna lily)
Lilium regale (regal lily)
Magnolia grandiflora (southern magnolia)
Michelia figo (banana shrub)
Muscari spp. (grape hyacinth)
Narcissus spp. (daffodil, jonquil)
Nicotiana sylvestris (flowering tobacco)
Osmanthus delavayi (Delevay osmanthus)
Petunia × hybrida (garden petunia)
Philadelphus coronarius (sweet mock orange)
Phlox paniculata (summer phlox)
Plumaria rubra (frangipani)

Reseda odorata (mignonette)

Rosa spp. and hybrids (rose)

Syringa vulgaris (common lilac)

Tulipa spp. (tulip)

Viburnum spp. and cultivars (viburnum)

Wisteria sinensis (Chinese wisteria)

Wisteria venusta (silky wisteria)

Aromatic Foliage

Abies balsamea (balsam fir)

Allium tuberosum (garlic cloves)

Aloysia triphylla (lemon verbena)

Angelica archangelica (angelica)

Anthemis lactiflora (chamomile)

Artemisia dracunculus (tarragon)

Dictamnus albus (gas plant)

Hyssopus officinalis (hyssop)

Laurus nobilis (sweet bay)

Lavandula spica (lavender)

Monarda didyma (bee balm)

Ocimum basilicum (basil)

Origanum majorana (sweet marjoram)

Pelargonium crispum (lemon-scented geranium)

Pelargonium graveolens (rose geranium)

Pelargonium nervosum (lime-scented geranium)

Pelargonium tomentosum (peppermint geranium)

Rosmarinus officinalis (rosemary)

Satureia hortensis (summer savory)

Satureia montana (winter savory)

Tagetes tenuifolia (marigold)

Thuja plicata (western red cedar)

Thymus citriodorus (lemon thyme)

Thymus vulgaris (common thyme)

Tulipa spp.

Lathyrus odoratus

Philadelphus coronarius

Pelargonium graveolens

SHRUBS AND TREES

Courtyards and patios are small-scale planting sites, and with the exception of perimeter beds, where taller-growing material can be located without appearing out of place, selections should be limited to dwarf and semidwarf shrubs and trees. There are scores of deciduous and evergreen species you can use that will provide privacy screening and seasonal shade without ever growing to out-of-scale heights.

Even some standard trees that mature at 40 feet (12m) or taller can be headed back periodically to check their upward growth. Usually, this forces energy back into lower branches and produces a fuller, bushier specimen. Your local nursery can advise you on which species respond well to this technique.

Following are lists of trees and shrubs that are proven performers in the residential landscape. In many cases there are dwarf forms available, which are ideal for small-space gardens. These may reach only 3 to 4 feet (90 to 120cm), while their parent species generally grow considerably taller. These smaller cultivars are often perfect candidates for containers and planters.

Don't overlook shrubs and trees that originated in your geographical region. These native species will adapt more readily to your soil and site and will establish themselves quickly in your garden.

Cornus spp.

Trees for Small Spaces

NAME	DECIDUOUS OR EVERGREEN	HEIGHT	BLOOM TIME
Acer palmatum (Japanese maple)	Deciduous	15'–25' (4.5–7.5m)	No bloom
Amelanchier alnifolia (saskatoon)	Deciduous/evergreen+	15'–20' (4.5–6m)	Spring
Cercis canadensis (eastern redbud)	Deciduous	25'–30' (7.5–9m)	Spring
Chamaecyparis lawsonii (in variety) (false cypress)	Evergreen	8'–30' (2.4–9m)*	No bloom
Chionanthus virginicus (fringe tree)	Deciduous	25'–30' (7.5–9m)	Late spring
Cornus spp. (in variety) (dogwood)	Deciduous	7'–30' (2–9m)*	Spring
Crataegus laevigata (English hawthorn)	Deciduous	18'–25' (5.5–7.5m)	Late spring
Crataegus lavelii (lavelle hawthorn)	Deciduous	15'–25' (4.5–7.5m)	Late spring
Cryptomeria japonica (in variety) (Japanese cryptomeria)	Evergreen	1'–60'* (30cm–18m)	No bloom

NAME	DECIDUOUS OR EVERGREEN	HEIGHT	BLOOM TIME
Halesia carolina (silverbell)	Deciduous	25'–30' (7.5–9m)	Midspring
Halesia monticola (mountain silverbell)	Deciduous	40'–60' (12–18m)	Midspring
Magnolia grandiflora 'Edith Bogue' (southern magnolia)	Evergreen	20'–35' (6–10.5m)	Late spring
Magnolia grandiflora 'St. Mary' (southern magnolia)	Evergreen	20'–35' (6–10.5m)	Late spring
Magnolia soulangiana (saucer magnolia)	Deciduous	20'–25' (6–7.5m)	Midspring
Malus spp. (in variety) (crabapple)	Deciduous	15'–35' (4.5–10.5m)*	Spring
Picea pungens 'Fat Albert' (Colorado spruce)	Evergreen	10'–15' (3–4.5m)	No bloom
Prunus spp. (in variety) (ornamental cherry, peach, plum)	Deciduous	10'–30' (3–9m)	Spring
Styrax japonicus (Japanese snowball, snowdrop)	Deciduous	25'–30' (7.5–9m)	Early summer
Thuja occidentalis spp. (in variety)	Evergreen	2'–25' (60cm–7.5m)*	No bloom

+ Depending on climate * Depending on variety

Cercis canadensis

Halesia carolina

Magnolia soulangiana

Prunus spp.

Shrubs for Small Spaces

NAME	DECIDUOUS OR EVERGREEN	HEIGHT	BLOOM TIME
Abelia grandiflora 'Edward Goucher' (Goucher abelia)	Deciduous/evergreen+	3'–5' (90cm–150cm)	Summer
Berberis thunbergii 'Atropurpurea' (red-leaf barberry)	Deciduous	4'–6' (1.2–1.5m)	No bloom
Buddleia spp. (in variety) (butterfly bush)	Deciduous	8'–12' (2.4–3.6m)	Spring–summer
Buxus sempervirens (English boxwood)	Evergreen	15'–20' (4.5–6m)	No bloom
Camellia japonica (Japanese camellia)	Evergreen	8'–18' (2.4–5.5m)	Spring–summer
Chaenomeles spp. (flowering quince)	Deciduous	6'–10' (1.8–3m)	Early spring
Cotoneaster spp. (in variety) (cotoneaster)	Deciduous/evergreen+*	1'–10' (30cm–3m)*	No bloom
Daphne burkwoodii (Burkwood daphne)	Evergreen	3'–4' (90–120cm)	Late spring/summer
Forsythia intermedia (forsythia)	Deciduous	7'–10' (2–3m)	Early spring
Hydrangea macrophylla (bigleaf hydrangea)	Deciduous	4'–8' (1.2–2.4m)	Summer–autumn
Hydrangea quercifolia (oakleaf hydrangea)	Deciduous	5'–6' (1.5–1.8m)	Summer
Ilex aquifolium (dwarf species) (English holly)	Evergreen	4'–8' (1.2–2.4m)*	No bloom
Ilex crenata (Japanese holly)	Evergreen	4'–8' (1.2m–2.4m)	No bloom

Chaenomeles spp.

Forsythia intermedia

Hydrangea macrophylla

NAME	DECIDUOUS OR EVERGREEN	HEIGHT	BLOOM TIME
Juniperus spp. (in variety) (junipers)	Evergreen	1'–12' (30cm–3.6m)*	No bloom
Lagerstroemia indica (crape myrtle)	Deciduous	6'–30' (1.8–9m)*	Summer–autumn
Mahonia aquifolium (Oregon grape)	Evergreen	3'–6' (90–180cm)	No bloom
Photinia × fraseri (Fraser photinia)	Evergreen	10'–15' (3–4.5m)	Early spring
Pieris japonica (lily-of-the-valley shrub)	Evergreen	8'–10' (2.4–3m)	Early spring
Pittosporum undulatum (Victorian box)	Evergreen	10'–20' (3–6m)	Early spring
Pyracantha coccinea (scarlet firethorn)	Evergreen	8'–10' (2.4–3m)	Early spring
Rhododendron spp. (azalea, rhododendron)	Deciduous/evergreen+	1'–25' (30cm–7.5m)*	Spring
Rosa spp. (in variety) (rose)	Deciduous/evergreen+	2'–10' (60cm–3m)*	Spring–autumn
Spiraea spp. (in variety) (spiraea)	Deciduous	2'–6' (60–180cm)*	Spring–autumn
Syringa vulgaris (common lilac)	Deciduous	6'–20' (1.8–6m)*	Spring–summer
Viburnum spp. (in variety) (viburnum)	Deciduous/evergreen*	4'–20' (1.2–6m)*	Spring–summer
Weigela spp. (weigela)	Deciduous	2'–6' (60–180cm)*	Spring–summer

+ Depending on climate
* Depending on cultivar

Lagerstroemia indica

Pieris japonica

Pyracantha coccinea

CHAPTER FOUR

CONTAINER GARDENS

PATIOS, COURTYARDS, AND OTHER OUT-

DOOR ROOMS COME ALIVE WITH COLOR,

GREENERY, AND AROMA WHEN AN

INVITING ARRAY OF PLANTS IS GROWN

IN CONTAINERS.

When combined with perimeter color, containers of flowering plants can be used to create a sense of a much larger garden in a limited space.

An interesting pot decked with cherubs and garlands is tucked into a niche to provide a charming garden accent.

Some of our friends have no facility in which to grow the plants they love other than pots, tubs, and troughs on their city decks and terraces. Others have space but no time for a conventional garden, yet they can always spare a few hours to fashion and maintain beautiful containers for their entryways and patios. These gardeners have become proficient in container planting, and it seems there is nothing they won't shove in a pot and coax to perform as well as if it were anchored in the ground.

Contained gardens offer many advantages. For one, they enable those who live in regions with frigid winters and frequent frosts to grow tender ornamentals that prosper in subtropical climates—citrus, Japanese camellias, and palms, for example. These cold-sensitive species can be spirited indoors before the first frost, then returned to the patio or terrace in the spring. Another benefit is that pots may be placed wherever you desire a splash of color or a touch of greenery. One favored spot is flanking the entry door.

As with traditional gardens, containers can be designed for full-sun situations, where most flowering and succulent species thrive, or for shady nooks, where you must take care to select from among a broad range of shade-tolerant plants. Consult the plant lists in this chapter for specific recommendations, but don't overlook local favorites and native species. Growing handsome

Corner accents can be created by combining several containers brimming with blooms—the flower display can change with the seasons. When this space is mostly shady later in the year, colorful foliage plants like coleus and caladium are used.

gardens in containers is probably the easiest gardening you can do—if you follow a few simple guidelines.

PLANNING AHEAD

Give some thought to what you want your container gardens to achieve. If you're looking for seasonal color to brighten up the patio or entry, you'll want to prepare pots of spring bulbs in the autumn. Follow these with early annuals such as forget-me-not (*Myosotis odoratus*), sweet pea (*Lathyrus odoratus*), and lupine (*Lupinus* spp.). After the annuals begin to fade, replace them with herbaceous perennials like false Solomon's seal (*Smilacina racemosa*) and wake robin (*Trillium grandiflorum*), then plant summer-flowering types such as phlox, salvia, and verbena, which will bloom into autumn.

For permanent patio or courtyard accents, consider woody perennials and shrubs. Options include those that bear flowers, fruit, or berries to provide added color and interest. Or you might choose conifers that are attractive in their own right—American arborvitae and mugo pine (*Pinus mugo mugo*) are two ideal choices. Broadleaf evergreen and deciduous species with striking variegated foliage also make bold statements. Some to consider are gold dust plant (*Aucuba japonica* 'Gold Dust'); *Buxus sempervirens* 'Elegantissima'; variegated forms of *Elaeagnus pungens*; *Daphne* ×

Amendments added to garden soil increase its absorption and water-retaining capacity, improve its fertility, and enhance drainage. Those shown here are all organic additives.

burkwoodii 'Variegata' or 'Carol Mackie'; and garland flower daphne, *D. cneorum* 'Variegata'.

To establish more vertical accents and screens, look to taller-growing shrubs or small trees such as upright juniper, holly (*Ilex* spp.), and bamboo. In mild-winter regions you might try camellia, ficus, or podocarpus.

CUSTOMIZING SOIL MIXES

The composition of container soil has a lot to do with how well plants grown in them perform. In addition to the pH level (see page 47), the other important consideration is the soil "recipe"—the ingredients that are combined to create the growing medium. Several national and regional sources market bags of planting media, and this is the most convenient source for container mixes. These mixes are called soilless mixes or synthetic soil formulas, and the best ones have been researched and developed at major universities. Depending on which product you buy, the mix contains several organic ingredients, including milled peat moss, ground limestone, perlite, vermiculite, sand, and wood products such as fir bark and redwood sawdust. Some packagers fortify their mixes with fertilizer, while others offer special recipes for specific plant groups—azalea mix, succulent mix, and so forth.

These commercial blends are lightweight, making it easy for plant roots to penetrate. Because soilless mixes are usually steam-sterilized, they are free of the common problems of garden loam, such as soil-borne diseases, insect larvae, and weed seeds. You'll find soilless mixes labeled "potting soil" under a variety of trade names in bags from 2-quart to 4-cubic-foot (1.9L to 0.1 cu m) capacity. If you have only a few containers or small planters to fill, this is the most economical way to go. But if you plan on filling large planters and containers, the most cost-effective method is to have a load of topsoil delivered. In most cities there are firms that offer this service, and many are listed in the telephone directory under "Soil" or "Topsoil." Unlike soil taken directly from the ground, commercial topsoil is usually custom mixed and composted.

What do you get when you buy soil from a bulk dealer? This depends on the source. Some companies offering topsoil are actually selling compost. This compost may be mushroom-based (the waste from a mushroom farming opera-

A pot filled with a good, rich soil mix ensures lush, healthy plants like these primroses, lobelia, and lobularia.

tion) or manure-based. Both are rich in nutrients and may contain some organic additives such as straw, sawdust, or wood shavings. Other companies may sell actual soil from construction excavations and other sources that has been enriched with organic matter and composted for months to produce a fertile mix that approximates garden topsoil.

It is fine if the only bulk mix available is compost, provided it has been aged, it is free of weed seeds, lead contamination, and disease pathogens, and you know what it contains. If you know the components of your topsoil, you can add amendments to blend special mixes. If the bulk soil you buy contains barnyard manures, it should be composted for a few weeks to dilute the potency and odor of the manures. Ask your source what ingredients are in the soil or compost and how long it has been composted. Proper composting usually kills most or all noxious weed seeds.

When you need a special soil mix formula or if you buy topsoil in bulk, you will need to add the amendments that create mixes suitable for what you want to grow (see box opposite for recipes). Many amendments are also used singly or in combination as mulches. Here is a description of the various amendments and what they contribute to a fertile, productive planting mix:

• **Compost** is decomposed vegetable matter that is filled with beneficial microorganisms and is very nutrient-rich.

• **Fir bark** is ground to a fine consistency and used to add humus to the soil. Look for bark that has been nitrogen-stabilized so that it does not draw nitrogen from the soil to aid in the decomposition process.

• **Leaf mold** that is ground so that it blends well with other ingredients is an excellent substitute for the costlier (and environmentally threatened) peat moss. Leaf mold performs a similar function, adding acidity and bulk, and is composed largely of ground leaves of deciduous trees.

• **Peat moss** comes from ancient bogs and is primarily decomposed vegetable matter that is high in acid content. It must be soaked before it is mixed in order to blend well and become water-absorbent. There is some concern on the part of conservationists that the world's peat bogs are threatened with depletion due to overharvesting by commercial interests.

• **Perlite** is volcanic rock that is ground and then heated, which causes it to expand to nearly twenty times its original volume. It doesn't absorb moisture, but moisture clings to its surface.

• **Redwood sawdust** adds to the structure and openness of a mix. It should be naturally fortified, not enriched with chemical-sourced nitrogen.

• **Sand** is composed of either quartz or mineral fragments and is excellent as an ingredient in mixes to help keep soil open for root penetration and efficient drainage.

• **Steer manure**, in addition to adding bulk to the soil, contributes some nitrogen nutrition to plants. Avoid manures that have been deodorized chemically, since these chemicals can damage plant tissue. With packaged commercial manures, deodorizing methods may not be recorded.

• **Vermiculite** is a mineral that, like perlite, expands to several times its original volume when subjected to extreme heat. It absorbs water and helps mixes retain their moisture content for longer periods.

Custom Mixes for Containers

Following are recipes for several general and plant-specific soilless mixes that are popular with gardeners.

Standard Mix for Annuals and Perennials

2 gallons (7.5L) finely ground peat moss
1 gallon (3.7L) compost
1 gallon (3.7L) sharp builder's sand
1 cup dolomite limestone
½ cup organic fertilizer

Standard Mix for Shrubs and Trees

2 gallons (7.5L) ground fir bark or nitrogen-stabilized redwood
  sawdust
2 gallons (7.5L) compost or fertile topsoil
1 gallon (3.7L) sharp builder's sand
1 gallon (3.7L) coarsely ground peat moss
1 cup ground limestone

Standard Mix for Herbs

Many herbs do surprisingly well in lean, unimproved soil, but like most other plants, herbs flourish in a medium containing fertile humus. In the main, herbs prefer a neutral or slightly alkaline medium that drains well. This mix has proven successful for many herb growers. (For growing angelica, lovage, and mint, add 2 cups of vermiculite to the recipe.)

1 gallon (3.7L) compost
1 gallon (3.7L) ground peat moss
2 gallons (7.5L) sharp builder's sand

Mix for Stone Fruits

Dwarf stone fruit trees need a mix that is lightweight and retains some moisture, yet drains well. To make your own blend, combine the following ingredients.

9 cubic feet (0.25 cu m) sharp builder's sand
9 cubic feet (0.25 cu m) nitrogen-stabilized ground fir or pine
  bark
5 pounds (2.2kg) organic fertilizer containing chelated trace
  elements
9 cubic feet (0.25 cu m) compost
5 pounds (2.2kg) dolomite limestone

Mix for Citrus Trees

Roots of citrus trees decline when there is excess water around them, so a mix that drains efficiently is essential.

2 gallons (7.5L) fir bark
1 gallon (3.7L) compost
1 gallon (3.7L) sharp builder's sand

Mix for Berries

Berries thrive in a humus-rich mix. Blackberries, blueberries, currants, gooseberries, huckleberries, and raspberries all do well in a medium that is somewhat acidic (4.0–5.5 pH). (For blueberries, increase the peat moss to 3 gallons [11.3L].)

2 gallons (7.5L) coarsely ground peat moss
1 gallon (3.7L) ground fir bark
1 gallon (3.7L) well-rotted (composted) manure
1 gallon (3.7L) sharp builder's sand

WATERING PROPERLY

It's safe to say that the primary cause of container garden failure is drought. A plant's need for regular irrigation is easily overlooked when the gardener has a busy schedule or takes vacations and other extended trips.

Plants in pots—particularly annuals and herbaceous perennials—may need water daily. During torrid spells in late summer, these plants may even need to be watered twice a day to keep them from flagging. To some extent, this slavery to the pot garden can be minimized by choosing only drought-tolerant or succulent species that can survive long stretches of aridity, but this usually limits one to a rather narrow palette.

If you have a schedule that is flexible enough to accommodate daily watering (early morning or late evening is best), then a good

Drip irrigation is the most efficient technique for watering plants. The emitters (shown above) inserted at intervals in the drip tubing direct a reduced flow of moisture around the root zone with little or no waste.

soaking inside the container rim throughout the summer will keep your container garden flourishing. It's best not to spritz with an overhead spray, particularly in shady nooks, because the moisture on foliage and blooms can promote mildew and rot. One exception to this rule is tough-leaved trees and shrubs, which benefit from a hosing off on hot, dusty days.

Of course, the ideal method of watering is with automated drip irrigation. This system delivers moisture to containers through lengths of spaghetti tubing and emitter heads in a slow, measured volume, which is controlled by a timer set to activate at regular intervals. The benefits include convenience, since the system operates automatically; efficiency, because the soil around the root zone is thoroughly soaked; and conservation, since there is very little water lost through evaporation.

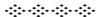

Window boxes spilling over with seasonal color can be used year-round for cheerful accents. Pinching off spent flowers regularly spurs more blooms.

Drip systems are easily connected to a hose bibb or to sprinkler heads and are relatively inexpensive. Do-it-yourself kits at most garden centers are priced under $100.

PLANTING AND MAINTAINING

One great advantage offered by contained gardens is that they may be established weeks earlier than it is possible to start a conventional garden in cold-winter regions. This is because frost and excess moisture in the ground must be gone before the soil can be worked. Seeds and plant roots deteriorate in cold, mucky soil. This is not a problem in planters and containers.

Although the air temperature in early spring may still be chilly and there may be a lingering frost threat, plants and seeds can be started in colder climates in containers filled with customized soil-

less mixes. When frost is in the forecast, planters can be covered with plastic or fabric attached to stakes to create a protective canopy; portable containers can be moved indoors or under a protective overhang.

Planting Shrubs and Trees

Many trees and shrubs, as well as some perennials, are available in containers or as bareroot plants. Some nurseries also package trees and shrubs as balled-and-burlapped specimens (often called B&Bs), which are similar to bareroot plants. Both B&Bs and bareroot plants are harvested from growing fields and greenhouses.

Plants purchased in tubs are the norm, and these are often the easiest to handle because they are actively growing when you buy and plant them. Knock the plants out of their containers and loosen any matted or tangled roots that may be girdling the soil. Match

them to a planter or pot of the appropriate size and simply drop them in, tamping in mix, if needed, to make a snug fit. Keep the topsoil about 2 inches (5cm) below the rim of the container. This leaves room for irrigation water to collect instead of washing over the rim.

Trees, shrubs, and perennials that will be sold as bareroot plants have the soil removed from around their roots. They are packed in sawdust, peat moss, wood shavings, or another moisture-holding material, then wrapped in plastic to keep the roots moist and viable while they travel to market. Note that these plants are shipped when dormant, so they rarely look very promising when they arrive, but most will flourish once they've been properly planted.

Top: Bareroot shrubs and trees benefit greatly from having their roots soaked in a pail of water for several hours before planting. This replaces moisture lost in transit and gets them off to a good start in the garden. Bottom: Bareroot bushes such as this rose are planted by spreading their roots over a mound of soil built up in the planting hole. This technique eliminates air pockets and ensures that the roots are in contact with the soil.

Balled-and-burlapped trees and shrubs are prepared in a slightly different fashion. They are dug with a soil ball around their roots, which will insulate and nourish the plant while it is in transit and during storage. Burlap is wrapped around the root ball and tied in place with sturdy twine.

Neither of these methods is better than the other, although bareroots are often less expensive and seem to adapt faster when planted. To plant bareroots, first carefully remove the insulating material from around the roots, and then examine the roots for damage. Any roots that are broken or decayed, or are too long to fit into the container should be snipped off with sharp clippers (dull blades crush tissue, and this can open the roots to invasion by diseases).

❖❖❖❖

*Many dwarf and semidwarf trees take readily to roomy tubs and can be grown in these containers
for many years. Adding colorful bedding plants around the tree creates a dazzling display.*

Terra-cotta bowls and a walled planter hold marigolds, ageratum, petunias, and phlox in a colorful array beneath a balcony.

After you've trimmed the roots, submerge them in a bucket of tepid, muddy water and let them soak overnight. This will replace some of the moisture lost since the plant was uprooted. The mud will coat the roots and seal them against any further dehydration.

Prepare a mound of soil in the bottom of a container; the mound should be high enough so that when the roots are spread over it, the crown (the point on the trunk where dark bark meets light bark) is an inch (2.5cm) above the finished soil level. Hold the trunk upright and centered as you trowel in the planting mix around the splayed roots. Firm the mix as you go, and when the container is half-filled, water to settle the soil. Then finish planting by filling in with the mix.

It's always a good idea to stake bareroots until they develop a root system vigorous enough to stablilize the plant in the container. Loosely tie gardener's plastic ribbon around the trunk and lash it to a stake driven into the soil 6 to 8 inches (15 to 20cm) away from the trunk. After the first growing season, the stake may be removed, since the specimen should now be firmly anchored in place.

To plant a B&B, remove the burlap that holds the soil ball together (when the tree or shrub will be planted in the ground, this cover is left intact to avoid exposing the roots, and it eventually rots away). After the cover has been carefully pulled away, compress the soil to firm it and set the specimen in the planter. Position the B&B a bit higher in the planter than you would container-grown stock. Because the soil around the roots is looser, it tends to pack down after several waterings and the plant will sink to about the right level.

Pruning and Thinning Shrubs and Trees

Studies in recent years have revealed that heavy pruning of newly planted shrubs and trees is not necessary and may even be detrimental to the health of the plant. Shrubs and trees need their foliage for photosynthesis. The only pruning that is recommended is to snip growing tips (except on coniferous plants) and to remove branches that are injured or crossing or that detract from the shape, balance, and proper branch structure of the plant.

There are two kinds of pruning—therapeutic, in which branches and stems are removed to correct a problem, and enhancement, in which cuts are made to promote more abundant floral or foliar development, to preserve the natural shape and beauty of a specimen, or to produce a special effect, such as topiary or espaliers.

Timing is the key to avoiding pruning problems, such as removing flowering wood too early or encouraging new growth too late in the season only to see it killed by ensuing freezes. Follow the schedule in the box below as a general rule of thumb,

PRUNING GUIDE

Type	*When to Prune*	*Comments*
Deciduous shrubs and trees that bloom before mid-May	When blooms have faded	FOR BLOOMS: This type blooms on old (last year's) wood Cut back stems or branches mid-May after flowering to a branch axis (where the stem joins the branch).
branches		FORCORRECTIVE PURPOSES: Take out crossing and all dead or diseased wood. Remove suckers at their source. Head back branch tips to control height and encourage fullness.
Deciduous shrubs and trees that bloom after mid-May	January 1 to March 1	FOR BLOOMS: These bloom on new wood (current season's growth). Head back old wood to a branch axis. FOR CORRECTIVE PURPOSES: Take out crossing branches and all dead or diseased wood. Remove suckers at their source. Head back branch tips to control height and encourage fullness.
Broadleaf evergreen trees and shrubs	Early May	FOR CORRECTIVE PURPOSES: Use same procedures as for deciduous shrubs and trees. Prune to rejuvenate shrubs and trees that lack vigor. Cut back growing tips (except on conifers) to force new growth lower down on branches. Take out some inside branches to admit light to the interior.
Conifers	Late autumn	FOR CORRECTIVE PURPOSES: Prune only to take out dead or diseased wood or to open up shrubs or trees. Hedging evergreens, such as yew and arborvitae, may be pruned and shaped, but most others are damaged in appearance by tip cutting.

Containers of color need to have spent blooms pinched or cut off (deadheaded) to keep pot gardens looking good and to encourage the production of new buds.

but bear in mind that there are exceptions, such as repeat-blooming rosebushes.

To avoid injuring shrubs and trees, make all pruning cuts with clean, sharp clippers, loppers, or saws. Branches that are removed must be lopped off straight about ⅛ to ¼ inch (3 to 6mm) from the trunk. A callus will form over this nub, sealing the injury. Don't leave a stub. These usually die back to the trunk and can open the door to decay.

In conventional pruning, cuts are made at about a 45-degree angle ⅛ to ¼ inch (3 to 6mm) above a dormant bud. You don't have to coat pruning cuts with pruning wound sealer. Gardening lore counsels this as a protection against infection and insect invasion, but this has been proven to hamper the callusing process.

Well-grown shrubs and trees may grow too tall for their tub or planter, but most should not be topped (headed back). When the leader, or main trunk, is cut back, the natural shape of the tree is destroyed and the tree compensates for the loss of its leader by putting out several of what are called epicormic shoots. These create an entirely different-looking specimen.

Branches may, however, be tipped by cutting them back 3 to 4 inches (7.5 to 10cm) to keep a tree or shrub shorter and fuller. A contained tree that is reaching for new heights will need to be transplanted in the garden.

Deadheading and Grooming

Flowering shrubs and trees, along with pots planted for seasonal color, will benefit from having the spent blooms removed as soon as they begin to fade. Plants spend energy maintaining deteriorating flowers and in setting seed, and this is wasted energy that could be invested in producing new buds or rejuvenating the specimen.

Containers, especially those close to the house, need to be kept groomed and free of blasted blooms and yellowing foliage in order to remain decorative assets. Seasonal color past its prime should be ruthlessly yanked out and replaced with fresh seedlings that will come into their cycle over the ensuing weeks.

Winter Care for Trees and Shrubs

Shrubs and trees are largely dormant during winter, rebuilding energy for next year's foliage, flowers, and fruit. Even in areas with mild winters, where gardening is a year-round activity, growth slows substantially until the advent of spring.

If your winters are severe, some of the ornamentals in your contained garden may need a little help surviving biting winds and frigid temperatures. Shallow-rooted plants like azaleas (*Rhododendron* spp.) can be damaged by heaving, which is caused by repeated freezing and thawing of the soil. After the first ground freeze, mound insulating material over the plant's crown. Use compost, straw, pine boughs, or ground bark for insulation, and cover this with plastic or burlap lashed to the trunk. Roses especially need protection in areas with harsh winters. You'll need to protect the the graft union—the point where the rose variety was grafted onto the rootstock—in particular.

At the end of the growing season, dormant trees and shrubs often need thinning and shaping. A good pruning job will enhance their appearance and performance the following year.

In areas where cutting winter winds are prevalent, it may be best to move containers of broadleaf and needleleaf evergreens to a shed or unheated garage, or wrap the branches in insulation and burlap or canvas. Exposed evergreen rhododendrons are probably the most vulnerable in frigid winds, which can shred their foliage, snap branches, and draw moisture out of the leaves. This moisture can't be replaced because the sap is frozen and unable to translocate through the tissues.

Applying an antidesiccant spray (ask for it at your local garden center) will help evergreens retain moisture in their foliage in blustery winter weather. These sprays may also be used to keep needles on both cut and live Christmas trees from drying out while they are indoors.

Young autumn-planted saplings and fruit trees with thin bark also need extra protection. Young trees in areas where seasonal winds are strong and destructive should be staked at planting time because their rudimentary root systems can't anchor them against strong winds.

A tangle of greenery and brilliant blooms creates a jungle effect in this verdant courtyard. Urns set on the stone floor and hanging pots add multilevel interest.

Smooth-bark maples and fruit trees tend to split from sunscald, a condition that results from the bark being warmed by the daytime sun and chilled rapidly during plummeting nighttime temperatures. Splits not only worsen through the winter, but also open the door to disease and insect invasion next spring. Protect smooth-bark tree trunks with tree wraps or a coating of white latex paint, which will reflect the sun's rays rather than absorb them.

Water trees and shrubs until the first freeze and during any winter thaws. While deciduous trees can usually survive without additional water until spring, evergreens dry out more easily because they pass more water vapor to the atmosphere through their pores. Without the extra water, the wind and cold of winter can cause dehydration of leaves and needles, giving them a singed or burned appearance.

Roses will need protection in areas where temperatures routinely plunge below 0°F (-18°C) in winter, but their hardiness varies widely by type and cultivar. Old-fashioned varieties are the most winter-hardy. Hybrid teas, floribundas, and grandifloras are the least cold-resistant. As with trees, it is important to prevent damage caused by heaving. If temperatures seldom go below 0°F (-18°C), you can protect roses by building an 8-inch (20cm) mound of soil, compost, or other mulch around the crown of each plant. In cold-

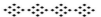

Left: Container plants can extend the color theme from the surrounding garden to the patio. This attractive lavender and white combination brings the garden right up to the house. Opposite: A potted garden every bit as appealing as a conventional in-ground one has been fashioned in a variety of lovely containers.

inal length and lash canes together with twine. Add mounding material as described above; once the soil freezes, cover the mounds with loose mulch and wire or netting.

CONTAINER OPTIONS

Without a doubt, the most popular container is the terra-cotta pot in its myriad shapes and sizes, which range from tiny 2-inch (5cm) cachepots to behemoths 50 inches (127cm) or more in diameter. Most plants seem to have an affinity for clay and thrive in pots made of this natural material. Popular styles include the standard flowerpot, which is usually twice as tall as it is wide at its mouth and has sides that slope inward toward the base. It traditionally has a thick rim that resists cracking if knocked over, but there are also cylindrical versions without a rim and with straight sides. These are commonly available in several useful sizes.

Azalea pots, sometimes called fern pots, are three-quarters as high as they are wide. These are ideal for growing shallow-rooted

er regions, build a similar mound, but cover it with a loose mulch of pine boughs or oak leaves held in place with chicken wire or nylon netting.

To protect less hardy roses in all cold-winter regions, strip foliage from the shrubs, water them well, and apply a fungicide just before the first hard freeze is due. Prune branches to half their orig-

plants that don't require the extra depth. The scale between these shorter pots and plants like azaleas and ferns is often more visually appealing. These containers are made in many convenient sizes.

Mexican pots, or ollas, are wider at the center and slope inward at the top and bottom. They are often decorated with designs etched into the wet clay before firing or are adorned with flowers and animal figures affixed to their sides. They are also thicker and heavier than most other clay pots of comparable size. Some are sundried and porous and will deteriorate after a few seasons. Well-made types are fired and last for years. Sizes range from small (about 6 inches [15cm]) to those large enough to house a small tree. Venetian, or Italian, pots resemble widemouthed vases in configuration and have concentric, stamped rings from base to rim. Many handsome versions are decorated with scenes from mythology or with horticultural themes.

Bulb pans or bowls are used for forcing bulbs, while shallow bowls are also used for dish gardens. These bowls are usually only one-third to half as high as they are wide. They are made in widths

AERIAL ACCENTS

Baskets of cascading ivies, ferns, and flowers have an eye-catching appeal that can transform a plain wall, drab patio corner, or commonplace entry into a spectacular focal point. You don't have to be an expert gardener to create these miniature gardens. If you plan well, you can make half a dozen in an afternoon or a weekend.

Assemble all the materials you'll require and lay them out beforehand:

• Wire baskets. Baskets come in a variety of sizes and shapes, including half-rounds for mounting against walls, posts, trees, etc. For ambitious gardeners, there are baskets that span 4 feet (1.2m) in diameter and probably require an entire weekend to complete.

• Sphagnum moss. If you plan to make only one or two baskets, buy your moss by the bag, but if you're going to do several, buy a bale. A bale should yield enough moss to line two dozen baskets 12 inches (30cm) deep and 18 inches (45cm) across. Leftover moss can be stored for future projects or used as an attractive mulch for potted ornamentals.

• Soil and amendments. You'll want to use the same lightweight soilless mixes recommended for containers (see page 60). One cubic foot (0.03 cu m) of soil will fill three to four baskets

(12 by 14 inches [30 by 35.5cm]). It is more economical to buy mixes in bulk than in small bags like those found in the garden section of supermarkets. At a garden center the standard 2-cubic-foot (0.55 cu m) bag costs about half what you'd pay for the same amount of soil in the "hobby-size" bags sold in supermarkets or other all-purpose stores.

For plants that prefer acidic soil, also mix in a quart (946ml) of leaf mold or ground peat moss (premoistened to enhance water absorption). If you're making a succulent basket, use a recipe of one part soilless mix to one part sharp builder's sand.

• Plant stock and seeds. For quick results, start with pony packs and starter plants from a nursery. You can sow some seeds for germination later, but these should be sown in the topsoil. They will sprout in the top of the basket, so leave room for them when you plant.

If you're going to put together several baskets, the least expensive stock comes in flats. You'll get two to three times as many plants for your money in flats as you do in pony packs. When choosing stock, pass up plants that are wilted or otherwise deteriorating. Start with fresh, healthy plants so that they can survive the shock of being uprooted and transplanted.

Plants for Hanging Baskets

If you're choosing plants for beautiful bloom and color, the following are ideal for hanging baskets.

Ageratum houstonianum (ageratum)
Begonia spp. (tuberous and bedding begonia)
Bougainvillea spectabilis (paper flower)
Browallia speciosa (browallia)
Catharanthus roseus (periwinkle)
Heliotropium arborescens (heliotrope)
Iberis sempervirens (candytuft)
Impatiens wallerana (busy lizzie)
Lobelia erinus (lobelia)
Lobularia maritima (alyssum)
Nemesia spp. (nemesia)
Pelargonium spp. (scented geranium)
Petunia hybrida (petunia)
Phlox divaricata (sweet William phlox)
Phlox drummondii (annual phlox)
Phlox nivalis (trailing phlox)
Phlox paniculata (summer phlox)
Primula spp. (primrose)
Tagetes spp. (marigold, dwarf)
Tropaeolum spp. (nasturtium)
Viola spp. (pansy)
Verbena hybrida (verbena)

Include some of the following plants for foliage and fillers.
Coleus hybridus (painted nettle)
Cymbalaria muralis (kenilworth ivy)
Ferns, including *Pellaea rotundifolia* (button); *Adiantum* spp. (maidenhair); and *Asparagus densiflorus* 'Sprengeri' (sprenger asparagus)
Hedera helix (English ivy)
Sagina subulata (Irish or Scotch moss)
Soleirolia soleirolii (baby's tears)
Succulents, including *Echeveria elegans* (hens-and-chicks) and *Aeonium* spp. (aeonium)

from about 4 to 24 inches (10 to 60cm), but larger sizes may be found in specialty garden or pottery shops.

Most standard types of clay containers are available in glazed finishes in a variety of colors. The advantage of glazing is that moisture, undissolved fertilizer salts (white encrustations), and minerals in tap water can't leach through to the surface and leave an unattractive patina. But this can also create a problem if plants grown in glazed containers are routinely overfed and overwatered. With unglazed terra-cotta, excess moisture containing some of the fertilizer residue is absorbed into the clay and passed through to the surface, where it evaporates. If you don't like the way your unglazed pots look, simply place them inside slightly larger glazed containers.

A suspended garden brings pretty plantings up to eye level in this charming moss-and-wire basket brimming with color. Pots and basket gardens can be hung from rafters or mounted on pillars and walls.

The excess moisture and salts still seep through the clay (which is beneficial to plants), but the result is not visible. Stains can be removed from clay pots after the plant has been removed by using a stiff brush dipped in a solution of one part chlorine bleach to four parts hot water, then rinsing with clear water. Make sure to wear rubber gloves and old clothing for this procedure.

Plastic and fiberglass pots, tubs, and troughs mimic the shapes of classic pots and tubs but are inexpensive alternatives to the pricier versions made of clay, stone, and metal. These newer materials have their advantages, but are not nearly as attractive or durable as the more traditional ones. Some gardeners prefer them because of their lighter weight. Others like the fact that they often cost about a third of what comparably sized clay or ceramic containers sell for. They

are available in a variety of colors, although the greens and earth tones are the least obtrusive.

A primary advantage of plastic over unglazed clay is that plastic is impermeable, and the soil in containers made of plastic or fiberglass stays moist much longer than it would in porous pots. This means less frequent watering, a real boon for those who grow plants that like having their feet damp, such as bog plants and many fern species.

Wood tubs and troughs are excellent for growing larger, deep-rooted specimens such as shrubs and trees. Traditionally, these tubs and boxes have been crafted from decay-resistant redwood, cedar, oak, or cypress, although less durable woods may be used if they are sealed and stained or painted, or if their interior is coated with a preservative compound such as asphaltum paint. Regardless of how diligent the attempts to preserve wood, it will eventually deteriorate and this decline is hastened by contact with water and damp soil. One way to prolong the life of wood planters is to use them merely to hold a specimen potted in a less attractive container, such as a plastic nursery tub.

❖ ❖ ❖ ❖

Exploding with spring cheer, these pots hold daffodils and tulips, which perform as well in containers as they do in garden beds.

To make the hanging baskets that will hold your creations, dip some moss in a bucket of warm water, squeeze out most of the moisture, and layer the moss in the bottom of the basket. To avoid skin irritation from the moss, wear rubber gloves.

Next, line the inside of the basket with moss up to the rim, keeping the layer about an inch (2.5cm) thick. Overlap thin spots so that soil won't escape.

Once the basket is lined, pour in a 3-inch (7.5cm) -deep layer of soil mix and firm it with your palm. Set in your first course of plants: poke a hole in the moss with your finger; take the first plant and remove some of the soil from around the roots; push the root ball through the hole in the moss; then pack some of the soil mix around the roots to hold the plant in place. Proceed the same way until you've completely encircled the basket. Then, move up a couple of inches and start your second course, and so on until the basket is finished.

Once the basket is completed, water it well and let it drain for half an hour, then hang it. Keep an eye on the moisture content of the soil. Moss absorbs water and causes the soil to dry out almost twice as fast as it does in clay or plastic pots. If your baskets are hung in the sun, they'll probably need to be watered every other day. The exceptions are succulent gardens, which can take the direct summer sun without flagging. Water these once a week or when the soil feels very dry.

To keep your baskets blooming for months, pinch out dead blossoms and foliage. This encourages vigorous new growth and enhances the appearance of your hanging garden.

Feed flowering and foliage gardens with an organic fertilizer a month after planting and monthly thereafter from spring to autumn. Succulent gardens require fertilizer only once a year, in early spring as growth begins.

Once floral baskets have faded in the autumn, remove the plants and soil and discard both. Save the sphagnum moss and baskets for use next spring, or plant the baskets with foliage plants to grow indoors during the winter.

Hanging containers other than baskets are available at larger garden centers and from direct-mail nurseries. Most popular among these are plastic or clay pots with either a built-in or detachable saucer and predrilled holes for attaching hemp or wire hangers. There are also metal clips that can be used to hang small to medium-size clay pots on a wall as well as another design that allows the pots to be suspended from a ceiling hook.

FLOWERING AND FOLIAGE PLANTS FOR CONTAINERS

Annuals

NAME	BLOOM TIME	COMMENTS
Antirrhinum majus (snapdragon)	Spring–summer	Good cultivars are 'Little Darling', 'Madame Butterfly', and 'Floral Carpet' (dwarf).
Browallia speciosa (amethyst flower)	Summer–autumn	Good cultivars include 'Blue Bells', 'Silver Bells', and 'Sky Bells'.
Calendula officinalis (pot marigold)	Autumn–spring	Dwarf strains include 'Bon Bon', 'Dwarf Gem', and 'Fiesta'.
Coleus hybridus (painted nettle)*	Summer	Does best in light shade. Try 'Carefree', 'Rainbow', and 'Wizard'.
Dianthus barbatus (sweet William)**	Summer	Good pot edger.
Iberis amara (hyacinth-flowered candytuft)	Spring–autumn	Needs some shade in warm summers.
Iberis umbellata (globe candytuft)	Spring–summer	Dwarf cultivars include 'Magic Carpet' and 'Dwarf Jewel'.
Impatiens balsamina (garden balsam)	Summer	Good cultivars include 'Double-flowered Dwarf' and 'Color Parade'.
Lathyrus odoratus (sweet pea)	Summer	'Bijou' is a heat-resistant bush type. 'Galaxy' is a summer climber.
Lobelia erinus (lobelia)	Spring–summer	Good for edging pot. Good cultivars include 'Cambridge Blue' and 'White Lady'.
Lobularia maritima (sweet alyssum)	Spring–autumn	Cultivars available in lavender, purple, and white.
Nemesia strumosa (nemesia)	Spring–summer	Good cultivars are 'Nana Compacta' (dwarf) and 'Carnival Blend'.
Petunia hybrida (petunia)	Summer	Pinch back to keep compact. F1 hybrids are disease-resistant.
Portulaca grandiflora (moss rose)	Summer–autumn	Good cultivars include 'Afternoon Delight', 'Wax Pink', 'Sunglo', and 'Sunkiss'.
Primula polyanthus (English primrose)	Spring	Prefers cool weather and some shade.
Salvia splendens (scarlet sage)*	Summer	Good cultivars include 'Fiesta', 'Flare', and 'Oxford Blue'.
Schizanthus wisetonesis (butterfly flower)	Spring	Set out after last frost. Prefers cool weather.
Tagetes spp. (marigold, French marigold)	Summer–autumn	Cultivars to try: dwarf 'Inca', 'Guys and Dolls', dwarf double 'Janie'.
Verbena spp. (verbena)*	Summer	Dwarf cultivars include 'Amethyst', 'Blaze', 'Rainbow', and 'Sparkle'.
Viola tricolor (Johnny jump-up)*	Spring	Self-sows.

Name	Bloom Time	Comments
Viola wittrockiana (pansy)	Winter–spring	Two good cultivars are 'Burgundy Lace' and 'Maxim Mixed'.
Zinnia spp. (zinnia)	Summer–autumn	Good cultivars include 'Buttons', 'Peter Pan', 'Ruffles', and 'Thumbelina', a dwarf variety.

* Annual or perennial, depending on the climate
** Biennial or annual, depending on the climate

Perennials

Name	Bloom Time	Comments
Aubrieta deltoidea (common aubrieta)	Spring	A recommended cultivar is 'Novalis Blue'.
Aurinia saxatilis (basket-of-gold)	Spring–summer	Excellent spreader.
Begonia semperflorens (bedding begonia)	Spring–summer	Long-lived; blooms in shade.
Begonia × tuberhybrida (tuberous begonia)	Summer	Try 'Nonstop' or 'Giant Cascade Double'.
Campanula fragilis (trailing campanula)	Summer	Use in baskets and window boxes.
Campanula isophylla (Italian bellflower)	Summer–autumn	Good for baskets.
Campanula porscharskyana (Serbian bellflower)	Summer	Does well in shade.
Catharanthus roseus* (Madagascar periwinkle)	Spring–autumn	Good for edging.
Dianthus plumarius (cottage pink)	Summer–autumn	A fragrant cultivar is 'Spring Beauty'.
Iberis sempervirens (evergreen candytuft)	Spring–summer	Compact cultivars include 'Little Gem', 'Purity', and 'Snowflake'.
Impatiens wallerana (busy lizzie)	Spring–summer	Months of bloom in shady locations.
Lysimachia nummularia (creeping Jenny)	Summer–autumn	The cultivar 'Aurea' has yellow leaves.
Nicotiana alata (flowering tobacco)	Summer–autumn	Good cultivars include 'Metro Hybrid' series and 'Sensation Mixed'.
Nierembergia hippomanica violacea (dwarf cup flower)	Summer	Two good cultivars are 'Mont Blanc' and 'Purple Robe'.
Pelargonium peltatum (ivy geranium)	Summer–autumn	Regular pinching of tips recommended. Try the cultivar 'Summer Showers'.
Primula polyanthus (English primrose)	Spring–summer	Prefers shade.
Tropaeolum majus (nasturtium)	Summer–autumn	Try 'Double Dwarf Jewel Mixed'.
Vinca minor (dwarf periwinkle)	Spring–summer	Propagate by cuttings or division.

*Annual or perennial, depending on the climate

Ornamental Herbs for Containers and Planters

NAME	TYPE	HABIT AND HEIGHT	PROPAGATION
Angelica	Biennial	Upright, 5'–6' (1.5–1.8m)	Seed
Anise	Annual	Upright, 18"–24" (45–60cm)	Seed
Basil	Annual	Bushy, 7"–48" (18–120cm)	Seed
Bay	Tree	Upright, to 30' (9m)	Rooted cuttings
Bergamot	Perennial	Upright, 24"–36" (60–90cm)	Seed
Bergamot, wild	Hardy Perennial	Upright, 18"–36" (45–90cm)	Seed, transplants
Borage	Half-hardy Annual	Upright, 12"–24" (30–60cm)	Seed
Caraway	Biennial	Upright, 12"–24" (30–60cm)	Seed
Catnip	Hardy perennial	Bushy, 24"–36" (60–90cm)	Seed
Chamomile, German	Annual	Upright, 18"–24" (45–60cm)	Seed
Chamomile, Roman	Half-hardy perennial	Bushy, 12"–18" (30–45cm)	Seed, cuttings
Chervil	Annual	Cluster, 12"–24" (30–60cm)	Seed
Chive	Hardy perennial	Clumps, 8"–12" (20–30cm)	Seed, division
Cicely, sweet	Perennial	Upright, 24"–36" (60–90cm)	Seed, division
Coriander	Hardy annual	Upright, 24"–36" (60–90cm)	Seed
Dill	Annual	Upright, 24"–36" (60–90cm)	Seed
Fennel, sweet	Half-hardy perennial	Upright, 4'–6' (1.2–1.8m)	Seed
Lavender	Perennial	Bushy, 12"–30" (30–75cm)	Seed, cuttings
Lemon balm	Half-hardy perennial	Clumps, 24"–30" (60–75cm)	Seed, division, cuttings
Lemongrass	Perennial grown as an annual	Clumps, 4'–6' (1.2–1.8m)	Transplants
Lemon verbena	Evergreen shrub	Upright, 3'–4' (90–120cm)	Transplants, softwood cuttings
Marjoram, sweet	Perennial	Clumps, 12"–24" (30–60cm)	Transplants
Mint, apple	Perennial/hardy perennial	Bushy, 24"–36" (60–90cm)	Transplants, cuttings
Mint, curly	Hardy perennial	Bushy, 18"–24" (45–60cm)	Transplants, cuttings
Mint, pepper	Hardy perennial	Upright, 12"–24" (30–60cm)	Transplants, cuttings
Mint, pineapple	Hardy perennial	Upright, 12"–24" (30–60cm)	Transplants, cuttings
Mint, spear	Hardy perennial	Upright, 24"–36" (60–90cm)	Transplants, cuttings
Oregano, Italian	Tender perennial	Upright, 12"–18" (30–45cm)	Transplants, cuttings

NAME	TYPE	HABIT AND HEIGHT	PROPAGATION
Pennyroyal	Hardy perennial	Upright, 12"–18" (30–45cm)	Seed, transplants, cuttings
Rosemary	Half-hardy perennial	Bushy, 2'–5' (60–150cm)	Seed, cuttings
Sage	Hardy perennial	Bushy, 12"–24" (30–60cm)	Seed
Sage, pineapple-scented	Half-hardy perennial usually grown as an annual	Upright, 3'–5' (90–150cm)	Division, transplants
Savory, winter	Hardy perennial	Upright, 8"–12" (20–30cm)	Seed
Tarragon, French	Half-hardy perennial	Bushy, 12"–24" (30–60cm)	Division, tip cuttings, transplants
Tarragon, winter	Half-hardy perennial	Bushy, 12"–24" (30–60cm)	Cuttings, transplants
Thyme	Hardy perennial	Spreader, 2"–12" (5–30cm)	Seed, division
Woodruff, sweet	Hardy perennial	Spreader, 12"–18" (30–45cm)	Transplants

Bulbs for Containers

HARDY BULBS

NAME	HEIGHT	BLOOM TIME
Allium spp. (allium)	8"–5' (20–150cm)*	Spring–summer
Chiondoxa spp. (glory of the snow)	6"–8" (15–20cm)	Spring
Crocus spp. (crocus)	2"–6" (5–15cm)	Spring–autumn–winter, depending on variety
Galanthus spp. (snowdrop)	9"–12" (23–30cm)	Winter–spring
Hyacinth spp. (hyacinth)	8"–18" (20–45cm)	Spring
Iris reticulata (iris)	3"–4' (7.5–120cm)*	Spring
Lilium spp. (lily)	1'–6' (30–180cm)*	Spring–summer
Muscari spp. (grape hyacinth)	4"–12" (10–30cm)	Spring
Narcissus spp. (daffodil)	12"–18" (30–45cm)	Spring
Scilla spp. (squill)	3"–20" (7.5–51cm)*	Spring–summer
Sterbergia lutea (winter daffodil)	6"–9" (15–23cm)	Autumn
Tulipa spp. (tulip)	12"–26" (30–66cm)*	Spring

* Depending on species and cultivar

Lilium spp.

TENDER AND HALF-HARDY BULBS

NAME	HEIGHT	BLOOM TIME
Achimenes spp. (magic flower)	18"–20" (45–51cm)	Spring–autumn
Agapanthus spp. (lily-of-the-Nile)	1'–5' (30–150cm)	Summer
Anemone spp. (windflower)	7"–15" (18–38cm)	Spring–summer
Begonia × tuberhybrida (begonia)	8"–24" (20–60cm)	Summer–autumn
Caladium spp. (caladium)	10"–12" (25.5–30cm)	Spring–summer
Canna generalis (canna)	18"–6' (45–180cm)	Summer–autumn
Clivia miniata (kaffir lily)	12"–18" (30–45cm)	Spring–summer
Crinum spp. (crinum)	2'–3' (60–90cm)	Summer
Cyclamen spp. (cyclamen)	4"–6" (10–15cm)	Summer–autumn
Dahlia hybrida (dahlia)	1'–7' (30cm–2m)	Summer–autumn
Eucomis spp. (pineapple flower)	2'–3' (60–90cm)	Summer
Freesia refracta (freesia)	12"–18" (30–45cm)	Summer
Gladiolus spp. (gladiolus)	2'–4' (60–120cm)	Summer
Gloriosa rothschildiana (glory lily)	3'–5' (90–150cm)	Summer
Hippeastrum spp. (amaryllis)	1'–3' (30–90cm)*	Spring–summer
Oxalis spp. (oxalis)	4"–6" (10–15cm)	All*
Ranunculus spp. (buttercup)	18"–24" (45–60cm)	Summer
Sparaxis tricolor (harlequin flower)	12"–18" (30–45cm)	Spring–summer
Tigrida pavonia (tiger flower)	16"–30" (40.5–75cm)	Summer
Zantedeschia spp. (calla)	18"–4'* (45–120cm)	Spring–summer

Caladium spp.

* Depending on species and cultivar

Cyclamen spp.

Shrubs for Containers and Planters

NAME	DECIDUOUS OR EVERGREEN	FLOWERS	HEIGHT	HARDINESS ZONES
Abelia grandiflora (glossy abelia)	Deciduous/evergreen*	Summer–autumn	3'–6' (90–180cm)	6–8
Berberis thunbergii (purpleleaf barberry)	Deciduous		4'–6' (1.2–1.8m)	4–8
Bougainvillea spp. (paper flower)	Evergreen	All year	Trailer	9–10
Buxus spp. (boxwood)	Deciduous/evergreen*		10'–20' (3–6m)	6–10

Name	Deciduous or Evergreen	Flowers	Height	Hardiness Zones
Camellia hybrids (camellia)	Evergreen	Autumn–spring	7'–45' (2–13.5m)*	7–10
Chamaecyparis obtusa (hinoki false cypress)	Evergreen		7'–10' (2–3m)	8–10**
Cornus mas (cornelian cherry)	Deciduous	Early spring	15'–20' (4.5–6m)	5–9
Elaeagnus pungens (silverberry)	Evergreen		To 15' (4.5m)	7–9
Euonymus europaea (spindle tree)	Deciduous		8'–20' (2.4–6m)*	3–9
Euonymus fortunei (wintercreeper)	Evergreen		Trailer	6–10
Forsythia spp. (forsythia)	Deciduous	Spring	1'–8' (30cm–2.4m)	5–9
Fuchsia spp. (fuchsia)	Evergreen	Summer–autumn	Trailer	9–10**
Hydrangea spp. (hydrangea)	Deciduous/evergreen*	Summer	3'–20' (90cm–6m)*	5–10*
Juniperus spp. (juniper)	Evergreen		Dwarfs, tree forms	4–10*
Lagerstroemia indica (crape myrtle)	Deciduous	Summer	To 30' (9m)	7–9
Lavandula angustifolia (English lavender)	Evergreen	Summer	1'–4' (30–120cm)	6–10
Mahonia aquifolium (Oregon grape holly)	Evergreen	Spring	3'–6' (90–180cm)	5–10**
Nandina domestica (heavenly bamboo)	Evergreen		3'–8' (90cm–2.4m)	6–8
Nerium oleander (oleander)	Evergreen	Spring–autumn	10'–30' (3–9m)	8–10
Osmanthus fragrans (sweet olive)	Evergreen	Spring–summer	To 10' (3m)	9–10
Photinia spp. (photinia)	Evergreen	Spring	5'–12' (1.5–3.6m)	7–10
Pieris japonica (lily-of-the-valley shrub)	Evergreen	Spring	To 10' (3m)	7–10
Pinus mugo mugo (mugo pine)	Evergreen		2'–10' (60cm–3m)	3–9**
Podocarpus spp. (podocarpus)	Evergreen		To 50' (15m)	9–10
Rhododendron spp. (azalea, rhododendron)	Deciduous/evergreen*	Spring	To 25' (7.5m)*	4–10*
Rosa spp. (rose)	Deciduous/evergreen*	Summer–autumn	Varies*	5–10
Spiraea spp. (spiraea)	Deciduous	Spring	2'–9' (60cm–2.7m)*	3–9*
Syringa persica (Persian lilac)	Deciduous	Spring	5'–6' (1.5–1.8m)	4–8
Viburnum spp. (viburnum)	Deciduous/evergreen*	Spring-summer	3'–20' (90cm–6m)*	3–10*
Weigela spp. (weigela)	Deciduous	Spring	3'–8' (90cm–2.4m)	4–9

* Depending on variety
** Except in desert regions of far western U.S.

Trees for Containers and Planters

NAME	DECIDUOUS OR EVERGREEN	FLOWERS	HEIGHT	HARDINESS ZONES
Acer buergeranum (trident maple)	Deciduous		15'–20' (4.5–6m)	5–8 (East); 6–9 (West)
Acer ginnala (amur maple)	Deciduous		To 20' (6m)	2–7
Acer palmatum (Japanese maple)	Deciduous		4'–20' (1.2–6m)*	5–8 (East); 6–9 (West)**
Cercis canadensis (eastern redbud)	Deciduous	Early spring	To 35' (10.5m)	5–8
Citrus spp. (dwarf varieties)	Evergreen	All year	7'–9' (2–2.7m)	9–10
Cornus florida (eastern dogwood)	Deciduous	Spring	8'–40' (2.4–12m)*	5–9
Crataegus phaenopyrum (Washington thorn)	Deciduous	Spring	To 30' (9m)	5–9
Eribotrya japonica (loquat)	Evergreen	Autumn	To 30' (9m)	8–10
Ficus benjamina (weeping fig)	Evergreen		To 50' (15m)	9–10
Ginkgo biloba (ginkgo, maidenhair tree)	Deciduous		30'–45' (9–13.5m)	4–10
Laurus nobilis (sweet bay)	Evergreen		12'–20' (3.6–6m)	9–10
Magnolia soulangiana (saucer magnolia)	Deciduous	Spring	10'–20' (3–6m)	5–10
Magnolia stellata (star magnolia)	Deciduous	Late winter–early spring	8'–10' (2.4–3m)	5–10
Malus floribunda (Japanese flowering crab apple)	Deciduous	Spring	To 25' (7.5m)	4–9
Malus sargentii (Sargent crab apple)	Deciduous	Spring	12'–14' (3.6–4.3m)	5–8
Picea glauca 'Conica' (dwarf alberta spruce)	Evergreen		6'–10' (1.8–3m)	3–6
Podocarpus macrophyllus (yew pine)	Evergreen		To 50' (15m)	7–10
Prunus cerasifera 'Thundercloud' (flowering plum)	Deciduous	Spring	To 25' (7.5m)	5–9
Pyrus kawakami (evergreen pear)	Deciduous/evergreen*	Late winter–early spring	To 30' (9m)	9–10

* Depending on species and cultivar

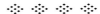

Vertical structures in the garden, designed to support plants like climbers and espaliers, contribute greatly to the overall design of the garden. In the next chapter, you will discover the value of arbors, trellises, and other structures that make a garden more appealing.

CHAPTER FIVE

ARBORS, TRELLISES & OTHER STRUCTURES

FOR MANY GARDENERS, THE LANDSCAPE

IS NOT COMPLETE WITHOUT AN ARBOR, AN

ARCH OR TWO, AND A FEW STRATEGICALLY

PLACED TRELLISES ON WHICH THEY CAN

DRAPE SOME OF THEIR OUTSTANDING

CLIMBING ROSES OR VINES.

A shady pergola is an irresistible lure on a sultry summer day. This handsome example will be draped with climbers in a season or two.

❖❖❖❖

A lovely arch frames a picture postcard view of this courtyard cottage garden. Note that the entry level change is color marked to alert visitors.

And for some plant fanciers, these scaffolds are indispensable in expanding the possibilities for greenscaping a tiny city courtyard or terrace. Going up is always a viable option when climbers are grown over trellises or tripods anchored in pots or planters.

Vertical structures in the garden serve two primary functions: first, they provide the upward thrust that well-designed gardens need, raising the eye above a single plane; and second, they furnish climbing plants with a sturdy framework that enables them to coil and weave to their heart's content.

ARBORS

The definition of an arbor has become a bit blurred in recent years. The classical description is a structure that is open on two sides. It usually has an arched top and often includes built-in seating. An arbor's walls are frequently lattice or of egg-crate construction, creat-ed by criss-crossing strips of lath. For practical gardeners, a sturdy arbor is an ideal structure for displaying heavier climbers such as roses and wisteria and offers a welcome spot to rest and view one's handiwork. For hopeless romantics, it is a place for trysts and flights of fancy.

ARCHES

Arches are sometimes mistakenly called arbors, but the two structures are a bit different. An arch is generally a single support with a curved top; arches are often used in combination to create a garden entry or a pass-through to another garden room. They're also picturesque when placed over a gate. Because they are not as strong as arbors, lighter, twining vines are grown on arches—morning glories and sweet peas, for example. Arches may be made of wood, wrought iron, or vinyl, which lacks the charm of old-fashioned materials but lasts indefinitely.

TRELLISES

Of all garden structures, none has more design variations than the trellis, which is probably the first plant support ever conceived. For the most part, a trellis design is chosen with two considerations in mind—the style of the house and garden where it will be placed and the kind of vine it will support. The most common trellis style is the lattice form, which can be installed close to a wall or fence. Fan trellises are popular in cottage gardens and against Victorian houses. To a great extent, the growth habit of the vine may dictate the trellis design. For climbers with tendrils or for those vines that coil, such as clematis and silverlace vine (*Polygonum aubertii*), a grid of sturdy twine is adequate. Heavier climbers such as roses and wisteria require galvanized or vinyl-coated wire to support their greater weight.

When considering a trellis design, remember that it should not overwhelm the climber and vice versa. A delicate annual vine looks totally out of place on treillage made of two-by-twos, while a vigorous woody climber like wisteria will tear apart a flimsy trellis meant for lightweight vines.

The most popular material for structural trellises is rot-resistant wood—cedar, oak, redwood, cypress, mahogany, and the less expensive pressure-treated pine. Vinyl trellises, introduced in the last decade, are also becoming popular. For purists, antique wrought-iron trellises have the most appeal but may be prohibitively expensive.

PERGOLAS

In early Grecian and Italian landscapes, the pergola—a roof held up by columns—was a favorite outdoor structure. In California and the American Southwest, the pergola is called a ramada. Pergolas provide a sheltered walkway or retreat, and are often covered with masses of vines. Unlike arbors, pergolas are usually built with very sturdy uprights and rafters, and can support even the heaviest of vines, such as grape and wisteria, both of which can twist apart flimsy supports by the second season of growth.

LATH HOUSES

As the name implies, lath houses are constructed of wood slats (called lath), which allow air and shafts of sunlight into the interior but generally create a cool, shady spot. Shade-loving plants in pots and hanging baskets can be grown inside during the hot months of summer, and large lath houses are popular for outdoor dining.

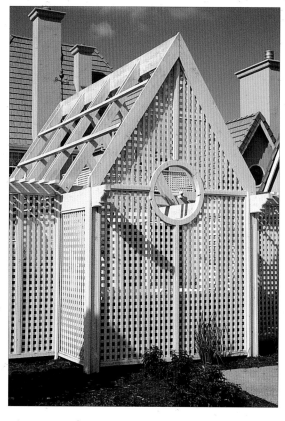

When covered with vines, lath houses add a festive and useful retreat in the summer garden.

WOOD FINISHES

When you buy, build, or have constructed for you any of these vine supports, you may want to color-coordinate them to blend with your house's trim or other garden structures such as fences or benches. Sealers, paints, and stains prolong the life of wood, which is continuously under attack from the weather; the sun's rays, rain, ice, and snow will all take a toll over the years.

When wood will not be painted or stained, sealers are generally used to protect it from moisture, although some stains are fortified with a sealer. While sealers won't provide 100 percent protection against the ravages of water, they do add years to the appearance and structural integrity of wood.

Paint is relatively inexpensive and quality exterior brands offer several years of protection. The problem with using paint on climber supports is that it is difficult to repaint the structures once a vine has covered them. If vines are stripped off after each growing season, this obviates the problem.

For almost every vine support, the ideal product for coloring and preserving wood is an opaque penetrating stain. A good stain will not flake or chalk and will usually outlast paint, which means that touch-ups and restaining will need to be done much less often.

Whether you opt for paint or stain, today's computerized color matching enables you to get the precise color you want. All you need is a swatch or 1-inch-square (6.5 sq cm) chip for the computer to analyze and produce a tinting formula for the mixer to follow.

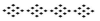

Above: Lath houses such as the one above provide a shady, private site for a patio. This one shelters a spa. Opposite: A handsome pergola and trellis provide the framework for climbing plants, which offer cooling shade to the house's entrance.

PLACEMENT OF GARDEN STRUCTURES

Arbors are versatile structures and, in the courtyard or patio, serve the same purpose as gazebos, which are usually too large to fit into such small-scale spaces. Arbors are rarely out of place no matter where you set them. In the cottage garden, they are often found at the end of a walk or path, but they can also be tucked into a corner or placed against a wall— they'll enhance virtually any spot where they won't appear out of scale with their surroundings.

Arbors may be placed virtually anywhere in the garden to fashion a romantic retreat, as seen in this small but charming courtyard.

Of all garden structures, trellises are the most useful. They can be used to dress up an unappealing fence, to create vertical landscapes against structural and landscape walls, to provide focal points for displaying handsome climbers, and as ersatz fences to break a large space into several smaller rooms. Smaller trellises sunk in containers enable the container gardener to grow a wide variety of vining plants in almost any location.

Although pergolas and lath houses are generally found in larger gardens, they can be scaled down to fit nicely in the courtyard or patio garden. Like arbors, they are

Arches seem most appropriate over a gate or walkway, or as an entrance to another garden room. Several arches linked together and covered with climbers can create a magical accent that lures visitors to stroll through them and discover what awaits on the other side. At the end of the path, set a special piece of sculpture, a fountain, or a flower-bedecked arbor.

most appropriate at the end of a walk or against permanent structures such as perimeter fencing or house walls.

All garden structures—particularly those within the confines of a courtyard or patio—benefit greatly from the softening effects of climbers and vines. In large measure, it is the appearance of twining greenery and colorful blooms that lends these accents their charm.

EVERGREEN PERENNIAL VINES

Some species will lose their leaves in subfreezing winters, then recover in spring.

Clematis armandii (evergreen clematis)

Euonymus fortunei (wintercreeper)

Ficus pumila (creeping fig)

Gelsemium sempervirens (Carolina yellow jessamine)

Hedera helix (English ivy)

Hedera helix 'Baltica' (Baltic ivy)

Hedera helix 'Bulgaria' (Bulgarian ivy)

Jasminum nitidum (angelwing jasmine)

Lonicera japonica (Japanese honeysuckle)

Lonicera japonica 'Halliana' (Hall's Japanese honeysuckle)

Rosa spp. (climbing rose)

Solanum jasminoides (potato vine)

Trachelospermumn jasminoides (star jasmine)

Deciduous Tender Perennial Vines

Akebia quinata (five-leaf akebia)

Asarina antirrhinifolia (chickabiddy)

Bryonopsis laciniosa (bryonia)

Campsis radicans (trumpet creeper)

Celastrus scandens (American bittersweet)

Clematis spp. (clematis)

Eccremocarpus scaber (Chilean glory flower)

Hydrangea anomala (climbing hydrangea)

Lonicera sempervirens (trumpet honeysuckle)

Parthenocissus quinquefolia (Virginia creeper)

Parthenocissus tricuspidata (Boston ivy)

Polygonum aubertii (silverlace vine)

Schizophragma hydrangeoides (Japanese hydrangea)

Thunbergia gregorii (orange clockvine)

Vitis spp. (grape)

Wisteria spp. (wisteria)

Annual Vines

Asarina erubescens (creeping gloxinia)

Cardiospermum halicacabum (balloon vine)

Clitora ternatea (pigeon wings)

Cobaea scandens (cup-and-saucer vine)

Dolichos lablab (hyacinth bean)

Humulus japonicus (Japanese hop)

Ipomoea alba (moonflower)

Lathyrus odoratus (sweet pea)

Phaseolus coccineus (scarlet runner bean)

Quamoclit pennata (cypress vine)

Thunbergia alata (black-eyed Susan vine)

Tropaeolum majus (nasturtium)

Wisteria spp.

Parthenocissus quinquefolia

Lathyrus odoratus

VINES AND CLIMBERS

Plants that coil, creep, twist, and twine their way up posts, pillars, and trellises or cling to walls and fences are indispensable in gardens of any size. They are particularly useful in softening the hard edges of walls and in making barriers friendlier.

The perennial vines you can successfully grow depends to some extent on where you live, although annual vines may be grown in any climate, since they are one-season performers. In areas of sub-freezing winters, the best choices are woody perennial vines such as wisteria and the 'Baltica' and 'Bulgaria' cultivars of English ivy *(Hedera helix)*. In areas with mild winters, there are legions of climber options, both deciduous and evergreen.

CHOOSING THE RIGHT VINE

Vines have developed a variety of specialized techniques for climbing, and to get the best results each has to offer, you need only match the vine with the support it prefers. Some are equipped with suction cup–like holdfasts that enable them to "walk" up a solid surface. These include English ivy *(Hedera helix)*, Boston ivy *(Parthenocissus tricuspidata)*, Virginia creeper *(Parthenocissus quinquefolia)*, and wintercreeper (Euonymus fortunei). All of these are happiest on walls and fences.

Twiners are the most common vining plants. Among these are Dutchman's pipe *(Aristolochia durior)*, American bittersweet *(Celastrus scandens)*, and honeysuckle *(Lonicera* spp.).

VINES AND CLIMBERS

Following are lists of vining and climbing plants grouped by their growth habit.

Clingers for Walls and Fences

Anemopaegma chamberlaynii (golden trumpet vine)
Campsis grandiflora (Chinese trumpet creeper)
Campsis radicans (trumpet creeper)
Decumaria barbara (false climbing hydrangea)
Euonymus fortunei (wintercreeper)
Ficus pumila (creeping fig)
Hedera helix (English ivy)

Hydrangea anomala (climbing hydrangea)
Macfadyena unguis-cati (cat's claw)
Monstera deliciosa (split-leaf philodendron)
Parthenocissus quinquefolia (Virginia creeper)
Parthenocissus tricuspidata (Boston ivy)
Philodendron spp. (philodendron)
Pyrostegia venusta (flamevine)
Schindapsis aureus (hunter's robe)
Schizophragma hydrangeoides (hydrangea vine)

Parthenocissus tricuspidata

Twiners

Actinidia deliciosa (kiwi vine)

Actinidia polygama (silvervine)

Adlumia fungosa (Allegheny vine)

Akebia quinata (five-leaf akebia)

Allamanda cathartica (loveflower-of-Guiana)

Aristolochia durior (Dutchman's pipe)

Asparagus asparagoides (gardener's smilax)

Beaumontia grandiflora (herald's trumpet)

Bougainvillea spp. (paper flower)

Calonyction aculeatum (moonvine, moon flower)

Celastrus orbiculatus (oriental bittersweet)

Clematis spp. (clematis)

Cryptostegia madagascariensis (rubbervine)

Dolichos lignosus (Australian pea)

Gelsemium sempervirens (Carolina yellow jessamine)

Hardenbergia violacea (lilac vine)

Hibbertia scandens (gold guinea vine)

Hoya carnosa (waxplant)

Humulus japonicus (Japanese hop)

Humulus lupulus (common hop)

Ipomoea spp. (morning glory)

Jasminum spp. (jasmine)

Lonicera etrusca 'Superba' (Etruscan honeysuckle)

Lonicera japonica 'Halliana' (Hall's Japanese honeysuckle)

Lonicera sempervirens (coral honeysuckle)

Lycianthus rantonnei (rantonnett night shade)

Mandevilla laxa (Chilean jasmine)

Menispermum canadense (moonseed)

Clematis spp.

Ipomoea spp.

Muehlenbeckia complexa (wirevine)

Periploca graeca (silkvine)

Petrea volubilis (purplewreath)

Phaseolus caracalla (snailvine)

Phaseolus multiflorus (scarlet runner bean)

Podranea ricasoliana (ricasol pandorea)

Polygonum aubertii (silverlace vine)

Pueraria thungergiana (kudzu vine)

Quamoclit spp. (starglory)

Solanum jasminoides (potato vine)

Stephanotis floribunda (Madagascar jasmine)

Tecomaria capensis (cape honeysuckle)

Thunbergia alata (black-eyed Susan, clockvine)

Thunbergia grandiflora (Bengal clockvine)

Trachelospermum jasminoides (confederate, star jasmine)

Vitis spp. (grape)

Wisteria spp. (wisteria)

Tendril Climbers for Wire, Twine, and Chain Link Fences

Ampelopsis aconitifolia (monkshood vine)

Ampelopsis arborea (peppervine)

Ampelopsis brevipedunculata maximowiczi (porcelain ampelopsis)

Anredera cordifolia (Madeira vine)

Antigonon leptopus (lovevine, coral vine)

Bignonia capreolata (crossvine)

Bryonopsis laciniosa (bryonia)

Cardiospermum haliacacabum (heartseed)

Cissus capensis (evergreen treebine)

Cissus incisa (ivy treebine)

Cissus striata (striped treebine)

Clematis crispa (curly clematis)   *(Continued on following page)*

(Continued from preceding page)

Clematis montana (anemone clematis)

Clematis paniculata (sweet autumn clematis)

Clematis texensis (scarlet clematis)

Clematis virginiana (virgin's bower)

Clytostoma callistegioides (Argentine trumpet vine)

Cobaea scandens (purple bell cobaea, cathedral bells)

Distictis cinerea (trumpet vine)

Gloriosa superba (glory lily)

Lathyrus latifolius (perennial pea)

Lathyrus odoratus (sweet pea)

Macfadyena unguis-cati (cat's claw)

Momordica balsamina (balsam apple)

Pandorea pandorana (wonga vine)

Parthenocissus heptaphylla (sevenleaf creeper)

Parthenocissus quinquefolia (Virginia creeper)

Passiflora spp. (passionflower, passion fruit)

Phaedranthus buccinatorius (flaming trumpet)

Pyrostegia ignea (flame vine)

Rhoicissus capensis (cape grape)

Smilax hispida (bristly greenbrier)

Vitis aestivalis (summer grape)

Vitis amurensis (amur grape)

Vitis argentifolia (blueleaf grape)

Vitis californica (California grape)

Vitis coignetiae (gloryvine grape)

Vitis girdiana (valley grape)

Vitis labrusca (fox grape)

Vitis vulpina (winter grape, frost grape)

Distictis cinerea

Vines and Climbers for Specific Structures

ARCHES

Species	Hardiness Zones
Actinidia polygama (silvervine)*	4–10
Clematis spp. (clematis)*	4–10
Ipomoea spp. (morning glory)*	3–10
Lonicera sempervirens (coral honeysuckle)*	3–9
Mandevilla laxa (Chilean jasmine)*	10
Menispermum canadense (moonseed)*	5–9
Passiflora spp. (passionflower)*	5–10
Phaseolus caracalla (snailvine)*	7–10
Phaselous multiflorus (scarlet runner bean)*	4–10
Rosa spp. (climbing rose)*	5–10
Stephanotis floribunda (Madagascar jasmine)*	9–10
Thunbergia alata (black-eyed Susan vine)*	4–10
Thunbergia grandiflora (Bengal clockvine)*	8–10
Vitis spp. (grape)	6–10

* Flowering climber

ARBORS

Species	Hardiness Zones
Actinidia chinensis (kiwifruit)	8–10
Actinidia polygama (silvervine)*	4–10
Antigonon leptopus (coralvine)*	8–10
Beaumontia grandiflora (herald's trumpet)*	10
Bougainvillea spp. (paper flower)*	9–10
Clematis spp. (clematis)*	4–10
Distictis spp. (trumpet vine)*	9–10
Gelsemium sempervirens (Carolina jessamine)*	7–10
Jasminum spp. (jasmine)*	8–10

Lonicera spp. (honeysuckle)*	4–10
Passiflora spp. (passionflower)	9–10
Polygonum aubertii (silverlace vine)*	5–10
Rosa spp. (climbing rose)*	5–10
Trachelospermum jasminoides (star jasmine)*	7–10
Vitis spp. (grape)	6–10
Wisteria spp. (wisteria)*	5–10

* Flowering climber

PERGOLAS

Species	Hardiness Zones
Actinidia chinensis (kiwifruit)	8–10
Aristolochia durior (Dutchman's pipe)	4–10
Beaumontia grandiflora (herald's trumpet)*	10
Bougainvillea spp. (paper flower)*	9–10
Clematis spp. (clematis)*	4–10
Humulus spp. (hop vine)	5–10
Lonicera sempervirens (trumpet honeysuckle)*	4–10
Rosa spp. (climbing rose)*	5–10
Vitis spp. (grape)	6–10
Wisteria floribunda (Japanese wisteria)*	4–10
Wisteria sinensis (Chinese wisteria)*	5–10

* Flowering climber

TRELLISES

Species	Hardiness Zones
Actinidia chinensis (kiwifruit)	8–10
Actinidia polygama (silvervine)*	4–10
Akebia quinata (five-leaf akebia)*	4–9
Aristolochia durior (Dutchman's pipe)	4–10
Celastrus scandens (American bittersweet)	4–9
Clematis spp. (clematis)*	4–10
Gelsemium sempervirens (Carolina jessamine)*	7–10
Lonicera spp. (honeysuckle)*	4–10
Mandevilla laxa (Chilean jasmine)*	10
Rosa spp. (climbing rose)*	5–10
Trachelospermum spp. (confederate, star jasmine)*	7–10
Wisteria spp. (wisteria)*	5–10

* Flowering climber

COLUMNS AND POSTS

Species	Hardiness Zones
Beaumontia grandiflora (herald's trumpet)*	10
Clematis spp. (clematis)*	4–10
Hibbertia scandens (gold guinea vine)*	10
Ipomoea spp. (morning glory)*	4–10
Jasminum spp. (jasmine)*	8–10
Kadsura japonica (scarlet kadsura)*	7–9
Lonicera spp. (honeysuckle)*	4–10
Schisandra chinensis (Chinese magnolia vine)*	4–10
Wisteria spp. (wisteria)*	4–10

* Flowering climber

Three factors that are as important as aesthetics in the creation of courtyard and patio gardens are privacy, safety, and security. We'll look at ways to achieve each in the following chapter.

CHAPTER SIX

PRIVACY, SAFETY & SECURITY

In today's hectic world, privacy is at a premium. When we are at home, we expect to be able to escape into the peacefulness of our private world. Making the courtyard or patio a sequestered retreat is an achievable goal in most cases, but the level of privacy that is possible varies.

Nightlighting not only lends a magical mood to the garden, it also reveals level changes and illuminates potential pitfalls after dark.

A solid fence topped by lattice panels provides a secure enclosure but allows cooling breezes to filter through.

A lot of your lighting choices will depend on the proximity of neighboring houses or buildings and the siting of your property. If, for example, your home is on the downslope of a hill, neighbors above will have a direct view into your yard and only portions of it can successfully be sheltered.

All things considered, this may not be a bad situation. In some areas, it may not be wise to completely block neighbors' views of vulnerable locations around your home. A curious or watchful neighbor may help foil prowlers or burglars who have targeted your home—but only if he or she can spot suspicious activity.

A compromise would be to select areas of the courtyard or patio that will be kept private and leave the rest of the space open to some view from the outside. The areas reserved for personal sanctuaries might logically be those devoted to sunbathing, a spa, or outdoor dining. You'll also want secluded retreats such as garden spots off the master bedroom and niches for reading and relaxation to be protected from view.

Privacy is attained in two ways—by planting view-blocking shrubs and trees and by erecting screens or other permanent structures that shield a portion of the garden. Shrubs and trees are much less costly than fences and walls, but there is usually a two- or three-season wait for plants to achieve the stature and width needed for them to be effective. With this in mind, you should buy the largest specimens you can afford. If you don't mind waiting a year or two, you should be aware that five-gallon (19L) container shrubs and trees grow faster than older specimens sold in boxes, and will soon catch up to more mature plants.

Also, look for plants in one- to three-gallon (3.7 to 11.3L) containers that are healthy and growing vigorously with roots just beginning to creep out of the drainage holes. These are often bargain-priced at the end of the summer and can be planted in autumn. Nurseries often move these small plants up to larger containers to sell at higher prices the following spring.

In early spring, shop for bareroot and balled-and-burlapped specimens. Be an early bird shopper for the best selection of stock. Don't let taller shrubs or trees mislead you into thinking they are the best choices. Your criteria should be trunk girth and branch structure. Short, stocky specimens will generally turn out to be more attractive and vigorous. With bareroot plants, examine the root development; sparse rooting means sluggish growth.

Following are some of the best shrubs and trees for hedges and screens. When considering plants, note that many are deciduous, which means they will be largely ineffective as screens and buffers during the winter months. If you plan to use your patio or courtyard chiefly in the warm seasons, the deciduous selections may make fine screens.

SCREENING AND HEDGING PLANTS

Plants 6'-8' [1.5–2.4m]

Abelia grandiflora (glossy abelia)*
Bambusa multiplex riviereorum (Chinese goddess bamboo)*
Berberis buxifolia (Magellan barberry)*
Berberis darwinii (Darwin barberry)*
Berberis mentorensis (mentor barberry)
Berberis thunbergii (Japanese barberry)
Buxus microphylla japonica (Japanese boxwood)*

Buxus sempervirens (English box)*
Cotoneaster acutifolius (Peking, hedge cotoneaster)
Escallonia rubra (ruby escallonia)*
Euonymus alata (winged burning bush)
Euonymus fortunei (evergreen euonymus, wintercreeper)*
Euonymus kiautschovica 'Manhattan' (Manhattan euonymus)*

Nandina domestica

(Continued on following page)

(Continued from preceding page)

Forsythia intermedia (forsythia)

Ilex spp. (holly)*

Juniperus spp. (juniper)*

Ligustrum japonicum (Japanese privet)*

Ligustrum japonicum 'Texanum'
  (Texas waxleaf privet)*

Ligustrum 'Vicaryi' (vicary golden privet)

Mahonia aquifolium (Oregon grape)*

Myrtus communis (true myrtle)*

Nandina domestica (heavenly bamboo)*

Prunus laurocerasus (English laurel
  cherry)*

Pyracantha spp. (firethorn)*

Rhaphiolepis indica (India hawthorn)*

Rhododendron spp. (rhododendron)**

Viburnum spp. (viburnum)**

Xylosma congestum 'Compacta' (compact xylosma)*

* Evergreen
** Evergreen or deciduous, depending on cultivar or location

Plants 8' [2.4m] and taller

Many of the following grow to considerable heights but may be kept under 10 feet (3m) by seasonal pruning.

Acer campestre (hedge maple)

Bambusa spp. (bamboo)*

Buxus sempervirens (English box)*

Camellia japonica (Japanese camellia)*

Caragana arborescens (Siberian pea tree)*

Carpinus betulus 'Fastigata' (upright European hornbeam)*

Chamaecyparis lawsoniana (Port Orford cedar)*

Cocculus laurifolius (laurel-leaf cocculus)*

Cornus mas (cornelian cherry)

Corylus avellana (filbert, hazel)

Crataegus spp. (hawthorn)

Cupressocyparis leylandii (Leyland
  cypress)*

Elaeagnus pungens (silverberry)*

Fagus sylvatica (European beech)

Ilex spp. (holly)*

Juniperus spp. (juniper)*

Ligustrum spp. (privet)*

Lonicera korolkowii 'Zabeli' (Zabel's
  honeysuckle)

Malus spp. (crabapple)

Osmanthus heterophyllus (false holly)*

Photinia fraseri (Fraser photinia)*

Pinus strobus (eastern white pine)*

Podocarpus macrophyllus (yew pine)*

Prunus laurocerasus (English laurel)*

Prunus lusitanica (Portugal laurel)*

Pyracantha spp. (firethorn)*

Rhaphiolepis indica (India hawthorn)*

Rhododendron spp. (rhododendron)**

Sophora japonica (Japanese pagoda tree)

Syringa spp. (lilac)

Taxus spp. (yew)*

Thuja spp. (American arborvitae)*

Viburnum spp. (viburnum)

Xylosma congestum (shiny xylosma)

* Evergreen
** Evergreen or deciduous, depending on cultivar or location

Prunus laurocerasus

Above left: This street-facing patio is completely shielded from view by a tall fence of narrow squared posts spaced to allow the passage of light and breezes. Shrubs and climbers on the street side provide additional layers of screening. Above right: Strategically placed screens of the proper height can transform exposed courtyards and patios into intimate spaces.

FENCES AND STRUCTURAL SCREENS

Unlike hedges and other living barriers, fences offer instant privacy and a measure of security. Used by themselves or in conjunction with plants, constructed barriers such as fences, low walls, and lattices are installed in courtyards and patios to contain, divide, and secure, and to block views into—and sometimes out of—outdoor spaces.

Fence and Screen Styles

The design of a fence is usually dictated to some extent by the architectural style of the house it will surround. Cottages and Victorian, Colonial, and craftsman-style houses go nicely with picket fences. Stark, boxy contemporary houses call for something a bit sleeker, such as a simplified wrought-iron fence, a board-and-slat style, or even a stucco-finished wall. Solid fencing offers the greatest noise buffer and privacy, but reduces the light level and

This basketweave-style fence is an example of a practical screen that serves as a barricade without blocking refreshing zephyrs.

blocks cooling breezes. These undesirable effects can be minimized by inserting lattice panels every few feet or by topping the fence with lattice or other openwork elements.

A solution that works well in brightening up the garden is to insert translucent glass or plastic panels in a fence. Neither privacy nor security is compromised, and enough light is transmitted through the panels to eliminate the feeling of being walled in. Another option is to install fencing that offers both privacy and security but permits ventilation. These styles include board-and-board (sometimes called alternate board), basketweave, and lou-

ver. An alternative is the lattice fence, which trades a bit of privacy for air and light penetration.

Fencing between properties should be carefully considered and, to avoid potential hard feelings, discussed with the neighbor who will be affected by its presence. In most cases, the best solution is what is called a good-neighbor fence, one that is attractive on both sides.

Used primarily to block outsiders' views into the yard, screens are also effective in hiding portions of the yard that do not always look their best—cutting and vegetable gardens, potting areas, and storage sheds, for example. Additionally, screens can be used to block unattractive views beyond your courtyard or patio, such as utility poles, a neighbor's clothesline, or any other sight better left unseen.

When plantings are not suitable for this task, you must resort to structural screens. These can be either solid or of open construction, such as that versatile element, lattice. Solid screens are easily constructed of exterior-grade plywood, but tongue-and-groove, rot-resistant dimension lumber is often used. To minimize their visual impact, you can paint or stain them to blend with your house trim, or—especially with lattice types—plant them with evergreen vines that will eventually create a

This security fence does its job without appearing too intimidating. It was erected around the courtyard to keep children and pets safely contained.

wall of greenery and, with flowering types, seasonal blooms.

MAKING THE YARD SAFE AND SECURE

According to statistics, more people are injured in home mishaps than by any other cause. With this in mind, give some thought to accident-proofing your yard to reduce the chances of injury to you, family members, and guests.

If there are children in the family, special care should be taken in several areas. Any water features and pools should be made off-limits to unsupervised children at risk of drowning. This can be done with portable fencing or safety covers.

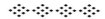

Far left: Rugged and beautiful, this security gate is electronically controlled. Note the intercom on the left pilaster. Left: A friendly-looking gate bids visitors to peek into the garden through its many convenient openings.

If small children will be using the garden, eliminate all plants that are poisonous or can cause rashes and skin irritation, and don't plant bushes that have sharp thorns. Even if the garden is intended for adults, thorn-bearing plants like roses and bougainvillea should not be placed at entries or along pathways, where they can snag clothes and skin.

Make sure to seal exterior electrical outlets with safety inserts to prevent children from inserting metal objects in them, just as you would with interior plugs. Gate latches should be placed out of reach of small children or equipped with locks. For both safety and security, gates can be locked and unlocked electronically with a remote control device. These are often used in conjunction with an intercom mounted on the street side to allow visitors to announce themselves.

Finally, if you have patio tables with glass tops, make sure these are made of tempered glass. Children are prone to climbing on furniture and, during their rambunctious games, could easily crash through a tabletop.

Steps made of the same tile or stone as patio floors tend to merge visually with flat surfaces. To prevent accidents, the lips of stair treads should be accented in some way to alert pedestrians to the level changes. One method is to use a contrasting stone on the edge of stair treads; the lighter stone should be noticeable even in dim light.

DANGEROUS GARDEN PLANTS

The plants in the following list pose a health risk, especially to children, who are naturally curious about the taste and feel of almost everything.

Agave spp. (century plant)—sap

Allamanda spp. (yellow allamanda)—all parts

Atropa belladonna (belladonna)—leaves

Brugmansia spp. (angel trumpet, datura)—all parts

Brunsfelsia pauciflora (yesterday-today-&-tomorrow)—all parts

Caladium spp. (caladium)—bulbs, leaves

Catalpa spp. (catalpa)—blooms

Catharanthus roseus (periwinkle, vinca)—sap, leaves, stems

Cestrum nocturnum (nightblooming jasmine)—all parts

Colocasia spp. (elephant ear)—sap

Convallaria majalis (lily-of-the-valley)—all parts

Delphinium spp. (delphinium)—all parts

Digitalis purpurea (foxglove)—all parts

Euphorbia pulcherrima (poinsettia)—leaves, blooms

Euphorbia spp. (various common names especially poinsetta)—sap

Ficus spp. (ornamental fig)—sap

Hedera helix (English ivy)—leaves

Hyacinthus orientalis (hyacinth)—bulbs

Hydrangea spp. (hydrangea)—leaves, buds

Hydrangea spp.

Ilex spp. (holly)—berries

Iris spp. (iris)—bulbs

Melia azedarach (chinaberry tree)—seeds

Narcissus spp. (daffodil, jonquil)—bulbs

Nerium oleander (oleander)—all parts

Parthenocissus quinquefolia (Virginia creeper)—fruit

Philodendron spp. (philodendron)—leaves, stems

Phoradendron serotinum (mistletoe)—seeds

Primula spp. (primrose)—leaves

Rhododendron spp. (rhododendron, azalea)—all parts

Ricinus communis (castor bean)—leaves, seeds

Robinia spp. (locust)—bark, leaves, seeds

Solanum dulcamara (bitter, climbing nightshade)—all parts

Solanum pseudocapsicum (Jerusalem cherry)—all parts

Taxus spp. (yew)—leaves, stems, seeds

Wisteria spp. (wisteria)—blooms, pods, seeds

Ilex spp.

Primula spp.

LIGHTSCAPING YOUR COURTYARD AND PATIO

One of the most effective ways you can make your outdoor spaces safer and more secure is by illuminating walks, stairs, and the perimeter of your home. From a safety standpoint, lighting will reveal level changes and obstacles that are obscured by darkness. You'll also achieve a greater level of security when foundation areas are lit up because anyone approaching windows or doors will be silhouetted or illuminated. Most prowlers will bypass a house that is very well lit.

Downlights, mounted out of view on a rafter, provide both security and accent illumination.

cookout areas, pools, and other amenities so that they can be enjoyed after dark.

Not too long ago, the purpose of nightlighting was primarily to deter prowlers, and the equipment available was designed solely for function, not form. Today, low-voltage exterior lighting systems are designed to create subtle and handsome effects with light and shadow, giving the landscape depth and dimension after dark. Even security lighting can be unobtrusive and low-key, yet every bit as effective as the megawatt high-voltage spotlights that are better suited to commercial applications.

There are a number of lighting

There are secondary benefits to nightlighting. It will enhance the beauty of your landscape by accenting and highlighting attractive features, and will make exterior spaces more useful by illuminating

effects that can be accomplished with the light lamp (bulb) and fixture. Once you've reviewed these, you'll understand how these effects can be applied to your own landscape.

✧·✧·✧·✧

This softly lit patio provides an inviting setting for outdoor activities on hot summer nights.

Downlighting

Any fixture or lamp that projects light downward is known as a downlight. The most common are shaded fixtures that illuminate paths, walls, and facades. Another technique, popularly called moonlighting, is a variation of downlighting. A fixture—usually a spotlight—is mounted out of view high in the branches of a tree so

that the light filters through the leaves to mimic moonlight. The effect is very pleasing and natural-looking.

Uplighting

Uplighting creates dramatic effects. Spotlights and well lights (floods or spots sunk into the ground) are used to illuminate the interior of interesting trees or shrubs. Uplighting may also be used

Just enough light has been provided around this spa for safety. Perimeter strip lighting under stair treads is particularly effective in lighting the way.

to project the structural patterns of plants against walls and fences, creating a dramatic effect called shadowing.

Background Lighting

Background lighting is used to illuminate walls, fences, trees, and other vertical objects, and can be accomplished with up-lights or downlights, or a combi-nation of both. Downlights are placed high in tree branches or under eaves so that only the effect, and not the source, is visible. "Wall washing" with light is an effective deterrent to prowlers since it eliminates shadows and hiding places around the perimeter of the house and reveals moving figures by silhouetting them against brightly lit surfaces.

Cross-lighting is used to add depth and to delineate contours in subjects like garden sculpture. Two or more up or down floods or spots are positioned so that their beams cross on the subject. A sin-gle light can be used, but the effect is not as dramatic.

If you have a pool or pond, you can create a nighttime reflecting pool with mirror lighting. This is done by illumi-nating trees and other features near the water so that they cast a reflection onto the surface.

Design and Installation Options

To install an effective lighting system, you can call an expert, such as a lighting specialist or electrical contractor, or you can do it yourself. Professionals will handle everything for you, from design to installation. Most pros work either on an hourly rate or for a flat fee. Designing and installing your own lightscaping is much more cost-effective, and it isn't that difficult, provided there are no power upgrades and con-duit work involved for 120-volt systems.

To begin planning your lightscape, find the courtyard or patio plan you made earlier. At dusk, take a long extension cord and plug it into a spotlight. Walk around your yard using the portable light

Handsome accent and walk lights, such as this copper tulip-shaded lamp, add a touch of elegance to the garden.

to see the effects the light creates in different locations and at various angles. Except in the case of walk lights, fixtures should be hidden; only the lighting patterns they produce should be visible.

When you're satisfied with the position of each proposed fixture, mark the location on your plan and record the type of fixture you'll need (well light, downlight, etc.). As you plan your system, use some restraint in the number and placement of fixtures. If you light everything, the magic will be lost.

Once you have a lightscape design in hand, you can install the system over a weekend. It's one of the easiest of all home improvement projects. Choosing low-voltage fixtures will make your task much easier. Most low-voltage fixtures attach to wiring with a screwdriver in seconds, and there is no danger of electrical shock because the low-voltage transformer that everything plugs into converts the power to a shockless 12 volts. Lighting kits generally come with easy-to-follow, illustrated instructions.

Low-voltage wires, unlike wires in a 120-volt system, don't have to be buried or encased in conduit because even accidentally severing them with a shovel won't cause shocks or short circuits. You can hide wiring in groundcovers, under shrubs, or beneath stones, bark, or wood chips for neatness, but the best way to conceal wires and eliminate the danger of tripping over them is to bury them in a shallow trench as you install each light. Wires that run to fixtures under eaves or in trees can be secured by carefully stapling them in place, taking care not to drive staples through the wire casing. You can camouflage the wires further by painting them the color of the house trim.

Unobtrusive lights like this redwood and lucite model are available from specialty lighting stores and through mail-order sources.

Since low-voltage lighting uses very little electricity, the average installation costs only pennies a night to operate. Most six-light systems use less electricity than a conventional 75-watt bulb. A 600-watt system—enough power to light a walk and perimeter-bed area—typically uses about four cents of electricity an hour, while a 1,000-watt setup consumes only about seven cents' worth an hour.

If you install your own low-voltage lighting, your cost will be nominal. With kits priced at well under $100 (and even less during promotional sales), you can lightscape both courtyard and patio, including some special effects, for about $300, depending on the fixtures you choose. Note that very pricey fixtures made of copper and other metals are available from upscale outlets. Each of these fixtures typically costs more than an entire six-light budget system. If price is not an important consideration, these are wonderful, well-made fixtures to own—but with a few exceptions, they provide no more illumination than lower-priced models.

More and more families are discovering the magic of water in the garden. In the next chapter, you'll learn how to choose the right fountain or water feature for your courtyard or patio.

A Primer on Low-Voltage Lighting Systems

Low-voltage lamps produce surprisingly bright illumination while consuming far less electricity than standard 120-volt floods or spots. A low-voltage system can simply be plugged into a weatherproof, step-down transformer/controller, which reduces household current to a safe, shockless 12 volts. The transformer itself is plugged into a ground fault interrupter (GFI), or grounded outlet.

Transformers/Controllers

Transformers with built-in controllers range from 44 to 300 watts at prices from about $20 to just over $100. The least expensive transformers are equipped with a manual on-off switch. Transformers with a photoelectric cell that automatically turns the lights on at dusk and off at dawn are the most widely used and provide added convenience, since you needn't be at home for the lights to work. These must be mounted outdoors to function.

Next in popularity are the time-clock models, which can be programmed to control the lights at specific times. Most expensive are the motion- and sound-sensor units used to operate security lights. Regardless of the type of transformer/controller you buy, a separate manual override switch should also be installed indoors so that you can activate or deactivate the system whenever you wish.

Lamp Types

A number of lamp types are available for low-voltage lighting applications. Incandescent lamps are similar in operation to standard A-type indoor lightbulbs. The low-voltage versions include A, R (reflector), ER (elliptical reflector), and PAR (parabolic aluminized reflector, or sealed beam) lamps. There is also a quartz incandescent lamp, which produces a light brighter than the preceding types. A recently introduced MR 16 quartz lamp has become an outdoor favorite with lighting designers. It projects a narrow, high-intensity beam that illuminates a small area, such as an alcove or doorway, from a distance.

Because of their cold color cast, fluorescent tubes are rarely used in landscape lighting but may be ideal for more utilitarian applications, such as illuminating house numbers, stairwells, and driveways. Warm white tubes are sometimes used as "wall washers" outdoors.

Fixtures

Fixtures are available in a variety of designs to fit virtually any application and budget. The greatest selection is in walk lights. The most familiar of these downlights are the tier or mushroom styles, which cast a soft, circular pattern of light on stairs and walks. Next in popularity are the flood- or spotlights used either to wash walls or as uplights under plants. A number of manufacturers make these fixtures, which can be found at most home warehouses and larger retail nursery outlets.

Several firms manufacture solar-powered accent, walk, and security lights that feature solar collectors. These recharge a built-in nickel cadmium battery on sunny days to produce from five to nine hours of illumination at night. Their biggest advantage is that they can be mounted in any sunny location without worrying about concealing wires or about their proximity to an electrical outlet. The biggest drawback is that during periods of prolonged overcast, most versions can't store enough energy to operate the fixtures for more than a few hours. However, manufacturers are working to correct this deficiency, and solar lights will probably be the wave of the future.

CHAPTER SEVEN

FOUNTAINS
&
WATER
FEATURES

A GARDEN POOL ADDS A SERENE AND

ALLURING FOCAL POINT IN THE HOME

LANDSCAPE. WHEN FILLED WITH AQUATIC

PLANTS AND FISH, IT CAN BE LIKENED TO

A JAPANESE GARDEN—A SCALED-DOWN,

INTIMATE VISION OF NATURE.

A well-planned water feature muffles street noises and creates a restful, refreshing vista from the patio and house.

Water gardens for small spaces can be tucked almost anywhere—one favorite choice is the garden wall. Here, a lion's head spouts into a catch basin.

Water—that most basic and vital of all the earth's elements—has an irresistible attraction for us. Feelings of tranquillity are deepened and troubled spirits are soothed. In a world of hard-edged realities and harsh contrasts, it is no wonder that water gardens are experiencing a resurgence.

Every year, more and more homeowners are adding a water feature to their garden. Some of these features are simple fountains tucked into a corner to create the pleasing sound of falling water. Others are small pools housing a few goldfish. Still others are elaborate ecosystems complete with waterfalls, plants, fish, and other aquatic animals.

offer an endless assortment of fountains, from the small, self-contained wall-mounted types to elaborate reproductions of classic French, English, and Italian styles.

Some fountains merely trickle, while others bubble at the surface, produce jets of water, generate a cascading effect, or combine jets with spillways in a lively water ballet. Many versions suitable for the small to medium-size garden are available at larger garden centers and from mail-order sources. They come pre-plumbed, prewired, and equipped with a recirculating pump that recycles the water. Little, if any, assembly is required, but you will need a ground fault interrupter (GFI) nearby to operate the pump.

FOUNTAINS

No matter how small the garden, there is space for a fountain. In response to the burgeoning interest in water gardens, dozens of specialty manufacturers have sprung up in the last few years to

For small courtyards and patios, the ideal model is the self-contained, wall-mounted style that has a spout above and a catch basin below, where the recirculating pump can be hidden.

Even these modest-size units produce a sound of falling water that is audible throughout the garden.

GARDEN POOLS

How much space do you need for a garden pool? We often see them as small as 2 square feet (1,858 sq cm). An extensive space is not a prerequisite for creating an enchanting floating garden in your courtyard or patio.

❖❖❖❖

Another small-scale water feature designed for a townhouse patio creates the alluring sound of moving water in less than six square feet (.5m²).

There are two important considerations to bear in mind when choosing a site for the water garden. The first is obvious—you'll want it situated where it can be viewed from the house. The second consideration may affect the pool's ultimate location: it must be sited where it will receive five to six hours of sunlight each day, away from trees that litter, and sufficiently close to a hose bibb for draining and refilling.

Formal pools are those rendered in geometric shapes—squares, rectangles, circles, and so on. Historically, formal pools have been installed either in gardens with rectilinear beds or to complement the grand formality of manor houses. Still, there is no reason why a formal pool can't be used in any setting, provided it is in scale with its surroundings and in keeping with the prevailing style of the garden. A pool's design, like art, is largely a matter of personal taste.

Informal pools can assume a variety of free-form shapes, but usually replicate the irregular contours of natural ponds and bogs. Charles Thomas of Lilypons Water Gardens once described an informal pool as having "just about any kind of outline. Through the well-planned arrangement of marginal plants, the informal pool appears to be a work of nature."

Just as with lightscaping, you can install your own water garden or contract with a professional designer or contractor to create a site-built pool. Two basic forms are usually offered—a concrete shell overlaid with glazed tile or other veneers, or a preformed, rigid fiberglass shell.

Professional help in designing and installing a water feature is available no matter where you live. Check the telephone directory under the heading "Aquatic Pools" or a similar classification. All landscape architects and most landscape designers are qualified water feature designers and installers. Architects and designers will usually work for an hourly rate or a flat fee. You may also choose to use a nursery or garden center that has a design/building department. Garden centers often waive the design and consultation fee if you hire them to put in your pool and furnish the plants.

You can, of course, design and install your own pool. Prefabricated fiberglass garden pools in a variety of shapes and sizes are available from a number of manufacturers (see Sources on page 141). Installing these shells involves excavating a pit that con-

forms to the shape and depth of the preformed pool. Most manufacturers of preformed pools supply complete instructions and tips for intalling the pool properly.

If you are especially energetic, you can make your own free-form pool over a weekend using fish-grade PVC (polyvinyl chloride) liner that is 12 to 32 mils thick (l mil = 1/1,000th of an inch), or the new, longer-lasting 30-mil-thick butyl liner. Keep in mind that the thicker the liner, the longer its life in most cases.

PVC liners have a life of up to ten years, depending on their thickness and a number of other factors, while fiberglass pools will last indefinitely, barring mishaps. PVC liners are, however, repairable if they are punctured. It's a good idea to buy a PVC patching kit when you order your liner. Many larger garden supply outlets also stock pool liners. Note that swimming pool liners are not suitable for aquatic pools since they are usually impregnated with toxic bacteriostats or herbicides to retard the growth of algae.

Installing your own free-form pool is a labor-intensive project, especially if you do the work without the help of heavy machin-

Designed and built by the homeowner in less than two weeks, this concrete-lined pond with brick coping is the focal point of her city backyard.

❖❖❖❖❖

*Built with seating-height walls for fish-watching, this pool was designed and constructed
by the artist-in-residence, who has filled it with aquatic plant and animal life.*

ery. Most of your energy will be expended when you dig out the pool cavity. Start by arranging your garden hose in the shape you'd like your pool. Score the outline with a shovel, then start digging the bed to the shape and depth you've chosen. If you plan to add fish, the pool should be a minimum of 18 inches (45cm) deep, although 24 inches (60cm) is the ideal depth. As you dig, add some ledges on which to set potted water plants. The top rim of the pool must be perfectly level. If the rim isn't level, one end of the pool will continually over-flow. To make sure you've got a level pool rim, place a long board across the pool and place a level atop it.

Once you have prepared the pit, line the sides and bottom with packed sand at least 2 inches (5cm) deep so that any protruding rocks or roots won't puncture the liner. Buy enough liner to cover the pool surface, plus twice its maximum depth. Lay the liner across the top of the pool and secure it around the edge with bricks or rocks. Then, use the garden hose to fill the pool. As the liner sinks into the pit, move the rocks back so that they aren't pulled into the pool but continue to keep the liner taut. The weight of the water will form the liner snugly to the sides and bottom of the pit without wrinkles or air pockets. Trim off some of the excess liner around the edges, but leave a border of about 6 inches (15cm). Anchor the liner at the rim by covering it with soil, rocks, or coping. Allow the filled pool to sit for a few days to allow chlorine in the water to evaporate, then add aquatic plants.

With the availability of the rigid ¼-inch-thick (6mm) fiberglass pool shell, whose estimated life is from fifty to seventy-five years, concrete pools may go the way of the dinosaur. When the price of materials for building a concrete pool is calculated, the cost runs about the same per square foot (929 sq cm) as a fiberglass shell, but the labor involved is roughly twice that of installing a pre-formed pool.

Another advantage of a fiberglass pool is that it is ready to plant as soon as installation is complete. A new concrete pool must be cured to rid it of calcium and free lime, which can otherwise leech into the water and harm plants and fish. There are several methods of curing concrete. One is to fill the pool with water and simply let it sit for a few weeks, then empty it, refill to flush, and empty again. This is the least satisfactory solution because of the time factor. One pool owner scrubbed the walls and floor of her new concrete pool with vinegar to release the lime, then flushed it three times before establishing her water garden. A faster method is to use a product such as Drylock Etch to neutralize calcium and lime.

One advantage to concrete pools is that you can have the precise shape and size you want to fit a particular space. Another consideration is that, for pools of 700 gallons (2,650L) or more, the cost per square foot (929 sq cm) is considerably reduced in comparison with fiberglass pools (which rise radically in price as the size increases), and preformed shells of comparable size may not be available.

WATER GARDENS

Garden pools that are correctly planted and stocked with the right balance of aquatic animals become what biologists call an ecosystem—a self-sufficient miniature environment. Each element in the water garden contributes to this natural balance. Balanced gardens are established by combining the appropriate plant species with the correct number and type of aquatic animals. The quantity of each required is determined by the size of the pool.

Two popular blooming water garden plants are the water hyacinth (left) and the water lily (right).

Water Garden Plants

There are hardy water plants that can, with special care, survive freezing winter weather. Tropicals prosper year-round in mild-winter regions; they can be grown above Zone 9, where winters are harsh, but they must be treated as annuals in most cases. Here's what you'll need to establish a healthy, balanced water garden:

• **Oxygenators** do more than produce oxygen; they also help reduce the growth of algae by competing for the same food and light. Fish often breed in their submerged foliage and goldfish get a valuable part of their diet from them. Some good oxgenators for the water garden are willow moss (*Fontinalis*), eel grass (*Vallisneria*), cabomba (*Nymphaeaceae*), and waterweed (*Elodea canadensis*).

• **Floating aquatics** help regulate water temperature by shading surface areas with their foliage. They float free on the water, grow rapidly, and are easy to separate from other plants for thinning and removal if they begin to crowd the pool. Among the best are water hyacinth (*Eichornia* spp.), water poppy (*Hydrocleys nymphoides*), water lettuce (*Pistia stratiotes*), and water aloe (*Stratiotes aliodes*).

Playful and easily tamed, koi are colorful additions to the garden pool and can be trained to eat from one's hand.

• **Marginal aquatics** grow with their roots underwater and their leaves and flowers above water. They are planted along the edges of a pool or pond. Popular choices are water canna (*Thalia dealbata*), pickerel weed (*Pontederia cordata*), and flowering rush (*Butomus umbellatus*).

Two of the most common pool plants—lilies and lotuses—don't fall into any of the previous categories. Lilies are members of the *Nymphaea* genus and lotuses are in the *Nelumbo* genus. These are the royalty of ornamental aquatic plants, producing bold, beautiful flowers and broad foliage that keeps the water cool, retards oxygen loss, and furnishes a haven for fish.

Fish and Other Aquatic Creatures

Aquatic animals comprise the maintenance and sanitation crew of the water garden, keeping the pool clear, clean, and functioning smoothly. Fish add an extra dimension, providing hours of diversion, especially for children, but also serving a practical purpose. In still-water pools, mosquitoes breed rapidly. Their larvae are one of a fish's favorite snacks. Fish also take care of most of the pests that plague water plants, including aphids and water lily beetles.

Four types of fish are normally stocked in a small to medium-size pool. Of the common goldfish (*Carassius auratus*), comets and shubunkins are the hardiest. Colorful Japanese koi or imperial carp, which often weigh nearly five pounds (2.2kg) at maturity, are easily tamed and can be fed by hand. Regal Higoi and Nishiki oriental koi carp eat aphids, mosquito larvae, and other nettlesome insects, but their primary value in the water garden is their exotic beauty and the endless hours of enjoyment they provide as they cruise their underwater domain. Golden orfes

(*Leuciscus idus*), surface darter and jumpers, have slender bodies and often grow to a foot (30cm) or more. Finally, in warm climates, various species of tropical fish normally found in indoor aquariums may grace garden pools.

The staff at Lilypons Water Gardens recommends stocking a pool with 1 inch (2.5cm) of fish to every 5 to 8 gallons (19 to 30L) of water, pointing out that this creates a better environment for growth and reproduction. Goldfish usually grow 1 to 2 inches (2.5 to 5cm) a season; koi and orfes can add 1 to 3 inches (2.5 to 7.5cm) a year.

Scavengers are important to pool maintenance because they keep the water free of debris and algae. These creatures include aquatic snails, such as the ramshorn (*Planorbis comeus*), black Japanese (*Viviparus malleatus*), and melantho (*Melanopis graellsi*), along with tadpoles, newts, and frogs. While scavengers do a fairly effective job of consuming insects and

Even a small water feature, such as this tiny court-yard fountain, can be effective in minimizing the clamor of traffic and other intrusive noises.

algae, the pool should also be equipped with a filter and pump, especially if it will be stocked with koi, which continually stir up bottom sediment.

Stocking a pool with a collection of about fifteen fish and some scavengers is not an expensive proposition, though the cost depends somewhat on the type and size of the fish you plan to buy. Note that there is a radical price variation among koi, which range from as little as $2 to more than $100,000 for a champion class specimen.

Hardy fish can winter safely outdoors in the pool, even if the surface freezes over. During long periods of freezing, a deicer must be used to keep an area of the water ice-free so that oxygen can get in and carbon dioxide can be vented. As temperatures drop in the autumn, fish will eat less and become sluggish. This is the time to stop feeding. Fish can survive the winter by drawing energy from their fat reserves.

Tropical fish and tender plants should be removed from the pool before the first cool days of autumn and wintered in an indoor aquarium until the weather warms around June.

Dining outdoors in pleasant weather is one of the great joys of having a garden. In the last chapter you will discover how easy it is to incorporate into a corner of the patio or courtyard a dining and cookout area you'll want to use all summer long.

ACCESSORIES FOR WATER FEATURES

Filters

Even an ecologically balanced pool may cloud up from time to time, especially if it contains fish. A mechanical or biological filter will keep the water almost crystal-clear and free of algae. Mechanical filters contain a pump and average less than $100, depending on the size needed, which is governed by the square footage of your pool. Mechanical filters will circulate the entire volume of pool water about every two hours. Removable filter pads trap impurities.

Biological filters are maintenance-free, but are much more expensive—from about $600 to $1,000. Impurities such as fish waste are broken down by bacteria in layers of gravel as pool water slowly flows through.

Pumps

If you plan on having a waterfall or fountain in your pool, you'll need a submersible or surface pump to circulate the water.

Electrical

Both filters and pumps require standard household current to operate. A GFI is recommended and, in many states, required. Typical codes call for the location of the outlet to be no closer to the water feature than 6 feet (1.8m).

Fencing

In some states or counties, there may be an ordinance requiring fencing around pools and other water features of a certain depth. Many counties in California, for example, require a permit and a 5-foot (1.5m) -high fence with a self-latching gate around any pool deeper than 18 inches (45cm). Check with your local building department for codes governing pool safety before you plan your pool. If you are having your pool designed and installed by a professional, he or she will handle the legal aspects for you.

Predator Control

If you have fish in your pool, there are only a few pests that may pose a problem, according to ichthyologist and waterscape designer Ben Crabtree. Cats, he says, rarely attack fish in ponds. Occasionally, raccoons, opposums, and blue herons do. One effective deterrent is nylon netting stretched over the pool. Once predators learn they can't get at the fish, they'll stop trying and the netting can be removed. Both raccoons and opposums are nocturnal hunters, so you can cover the pool only at night if the netting is visually unappealing to you.

CHAPTER EIGHT

DINING ALFRESCO

ONE OF THE GREAT ICONS OF MOD-

ERN LIFE IS THE BACKYARD COOKOUT.

MULTITUDES OF PEOPLE SPEND ENTIRE

SUMMERS SACRIFICING MILLIONS OF CHAR-

COAL BRIQUETTES AND OCEANS OF FLAM-

MABLE LIQUID TO THE GOD OF FIRE.

*Cooking and dining outdoors is one of the most popular summer
pastimes, akin to the elaborate family picnic of past generations.*

Protected from the elements, this outdoor room was designed for festive summer occasions and family get-togethers.

As dedicated barbecuers, we endure swarms of blackflies, hordes of ants, and squadrons of mosquitoes rather than prepare a picnic meal in the comfort of our air-conditioned kitchens.

Cookouts have always been festive affairs—an enjoyable way to get family and friends together for an informal meal. Over the last decade or so, technology has caught up with the passion for outdoor cooking, enabling us to prepare full-course meals without ever stepping inside the house.

sink, grill, and open-pit barbecue. In recent years, some outdoor kitchens we've seen have, in addition, built-in woks, dishwashers, and ceiling fans, purportedly to keep mosquitoes at bay.

These elaborate installations were once thought to be worthwhile investments only in the warmest climates, such as California and Florida, where mild winters mean year-round outdoor entertaining. But in the last few years families from all over have embraced the concept of an outdoor kitchen that is

OUTDOOR KITCHENS

Currently, the trend in outdoor entertainment features is toward the fully equipped outdoor kitchen, complete with refrigerator,

nearly as complete and self-contained as their interior version. Although it may seem extravagant to invest in facilities that can be used for only part of the year, when you consider the long, hot

Half of this airy poolhouse serves as a sheltered outdoor dining room. Note complete kitchen to the right.

summers during which no one wants to turn on the oven, the expenditure is understandable.

Siting the Outdoor Kitchen

No courtyard or patio is too small for a cookout center. One of the most compact examples we have seen is contained in an alcove against a house wall in just 8 feet (2.4m) of space and is camouflaged by folding doors when not in use. This barbecue is equipped with a natural gas grill, sink, small refrigerator, and upper and lower storage cabinets. Smoke from the grill is vented through a standard range hood vent, and during winter months and inclement weather, everything is kept tidy and dry. It is a marvel of efficiency and good planning and the family makes excellent use of its investment.

There are two schools of thought on the placement of outdoor kitchens. One philosophy holds that these outdoor cooking centers should be close to the house to minimize long treks back and

❖·❖·❖·❖

An outdoor fireplace extends the season for enjoying patios and creates a cozy gathering spot on cool evenings.

forth with food, dishes, and kindred paraphernalia. The other counsels that they should be located as far from the house as is feasible so that smoke and odors are isolated. Both locations have their advantages.

Certainly, on small patios or courtyards, the best place for a cookout center is out of the main flow of traffic. This means a site somewhere on the perimeter—unless you opt to place the barbecue against the house.

Sometimes the existing characteristics and features of the patio or courtyard will dictate the best location. For kitchens that will be equipped with appliances and sinks, the gas, electrical, and plumbing service lines will have to be run to the site. If the kitchen is to be located on a patio adjacent to the house, the lines serving the house can easily be tapped and extended into the outdoor space. If the kitchen is to be on a detached patio, the lines will have to be laid in a trench. Trenching under slabs and other hardscape is extremely difficult to do, so planning ahead can save you considerable time and expense.

One family, long devoted to outdoor cooking, installed two grills at their vacation home when they decided to live there year-round. One grill was placed in a gazebo some distance from the house and

is used for large gatherings. A smaller gas grill went on the patio against an exterior kitchen wall. "This is the one we use almost every day," the homeowner said. "It's so convenient on hot days to just pop out and grill a meal without heating up the whole house."

Equipping the Kitchen

First and foremost, the grill is the heart of the outdoor kitchen. A number of manufacturers offer built-in models fired by liquid petroleum (LP) gas, natural gas, or charcoal. The best grills are either stainless steel or steel overlaid with porcelain.

Two-burner grill begin at about $200, while deluxe six-burner styles with up to 660 square inches (4,258 sq cm) of cooking surface and 18,000 BTUs per burner may range well into the thousands of dollars. High-end styles offer the convenience of push-button ignition, flare protection, and commercial-style cast-brass or cast-iron burners.

❖❖❖❖❖

An innovative use of wall space was employed with this cookout center, which houses a grill, refrigerator, sink, and ample storage—all of which can be concealed behind folding doors.

Accessories will add to the ultimate cost of a grill setup. Useful to consider is the smoke oven, which fits over the grill surface and is equipped with a rolltop door. This allows you to infuse meats with a wood-

Barbecue centers located some distance from the house keep the heat of the grill, as well as smoke and cooking odors, at bay.

smoked taste. Other useful add-ons include side burners, which operate at a variety of temperatures; chrome warming racks; rotisserie kits; and poultry holders that attach to rotisseries to ensure thorough, even cooking.

This cookout center is conveniently located on the patio just outside the kitchen door.

Least expensive, and somewhat limited in features, are the charcoal-burning grills. Next in cost are the LP models, which are connected to a propane tank that must be periodically refilled. Costliest, but most convenient, are the natural gas–fired styles. These usually come with the broadest range of accessories.

Choosing the best grill for your outdoor kitchen is largely a matter of budget and the frequency of your barbecues. If you don't barbecue more than half a dozen times a year, you will probably find the old standby charcoal grill adequate for your needs. But if cookouts are a weekly occurrence in your family, you'll probably be most satisfied with an LP or natural gas–fired grill.

Outdoor countertops are subjected to a lot more abuse than their interior counterparts, and this includes weather that ranges from blazing hot to freezing cold in many regions. Counter surfaces should be durable and easy to maintain, and this means tiling them or covering them with some other hard surface material. Material choices should, if possible, complement the hardscape in the outdoor living areas.

If you use flagstone or another porous stone, it should be sealed so that cooking oils and grease are not absorbed. Once these surfaces are stained, it is difficult and time-consuming to restore their original appearance, although it can be done professionally.

Laminated countertops look great and are appealingly economical, but they are not intended for exterior use in exposed areas. Weather extremes will soon open seams and cause the laminated layers to separate. These countertops can, however, be used in weather-tight outdoor environments.

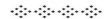

An elegant outdoor cooking area, installed against the house, has all the elements of a modern kitchen— refrigerator, sink, dishwasher, cook top, and ample cabinet storage and counter space.

Don't skimp on counter size to save a few dollars; your inadequate counter space will be a continual source of regret. Just as in a traditional kitchen, you need ample room to set up and to prepare and serve food. If the counters will double as dining space, they should be the proper height to accommodate standard bar stools. For the cook, the counters should be at the right level for comfort. Level changes can be used to create the proper counter height for diners and to achieve the ideal height for food preparation. This is most often accomplished by dropping the level of the cooking platform a few inches below the patio floor. Another solution is to reduce the dining counter to dining-chair height.

Storage cabinets should be made of rot-resistant softwoods like redwood, cedar, or cypress, or of moisture-resistant hardwoods such as oak, teak, or mahogany. While these durable woods are preferable, less stable woods like hemlock, fir, pine, and spruce can be used if they are sealed and stained or sealed and painted with two topcoats of enamel. Alternatively, they may be stained and given a water-repellent finish. In addition, veneered exterior-grade plywood and oriented strand board (OSB) may be used to build cabinets. Both are highly stable in harsh weather and damp environments.

Full-size sinks are preferable to bar sinks, which are often chosen (mistakenly, in our opinion) for outdoor kitchens. Bar sinks are too

❖❖❖❖❖

Left: This sturdy pergola features Lexan panels on the rafters to offer some shelter from the elements. A custom-made cover protects the grill and counter. Above: A light overhead provides some relief from the sun.

small to accommodate pots and skillets. Stainless steel lasts as long as porcelain and looks better longer.

Roof Coverings and Screens

Any outdoor kitchen that contains appliances such as a refrigerator, grill, or dishwasher must be protected from the elements by a solid roof. The typical roof is made of exterior-grade plywood or OSB attached to rafters, then covered with some type of roofing—shingles, shakes, etc. In areas where winters are mild, one often sees solid roofing made of lucite or glass panels so that

A covered and screened patio is the ideal location for alfresco dining. Lattice panels admit light and fresh air, yet provide a measure of privacy.

appliances are protected from rain and tree litter, but light is not blocked out.

For dining comfort, overhead structures should cover the table to create a haven from the sun. The overhead should be ample enough to provide some shelter for any benches around the patio.

For small areas, you may only need a couple of strategically placed patio umbrellas, which can be collapsed when not in use.

Cookout areas are often screened for privacy and occasionally to simply hide them from view for aesthetic reasons. The simplest way to handle this is to choose an attractive evergreen hedging plant, such as boxwood (*Buxus* spp.) or yew (*Taxus* spp.), and space plants at the proper distance to create a hedge around the area.

Two ideal structural elements for screens are lattice panels, which come ready-made in 4- by 8-foot (1.2 by 2.4m) and 6- by 10-foot (1.8 by 3m) panels, but can also be custom-made to your specifications. Both of these screening styles allow smoke and odors to escape while admitting light and air. They also minimize the feeling of claustrophobia that solid screens sometimes engender.

CAVEATS FOR HARSH WINTER CLIMES

Outdoor kitchens, complete with appliances, were once thought to be feasible only in warm climates. But homeowners in areas of seasonal frosts and freezes can also have fully equipped cookout centers as long as certain precautions against the ravages of winter are taken.

Knowledgeable plumbers and electricians know the threats posed by moisture and freezing temperatures to pipes, outlets, and appliances, and can take steps to avoid problems.

Pipes

Anyone who lives in frigid winter climates knows that water standing in exposed plumbing lines can freeze and burst the pipes. To avoid this, plumbers insulate pipes and install valves that can be used to drain pipes of standing water. Draining all exterior lines should become a standard preventive measure with the onset of freezing weather.

Appliances

Manufacturers have yet to produce all-weather appliances. Dishwashers, ranges, and refrigerators installed outdoors need protection against the elements. This includes a leak-free roof and shielding from wind-driven rain, snow, and sleet by enclosing them in or between cabinets, counters, and the like and sheltering them with weatherproof covers.

Both animals and insects can wreck wiring and other vulnerable parts, so some precautions need to be taken to protect appliances from these perils. It's usually a sound idea to install a lock on refrigerators and cabinets as a safety precaution and to deny access to foraging animals. Raccoons have been known to quickly get the knack of opening doors to get at stored provisions.

Electrical

To avoid shocks, short circuits, electrical fires, and damage to appliances or tools, all exterior outlets should be wired to a ground fault interrupter (GFI), sometimes called a ground fault circuit interrupter (GFCI). A separate circuit-breaker line to service these utility areas is ideal, as it allows you to shut off power to the lines for the winter.

PLANT HARDINESS ZONES

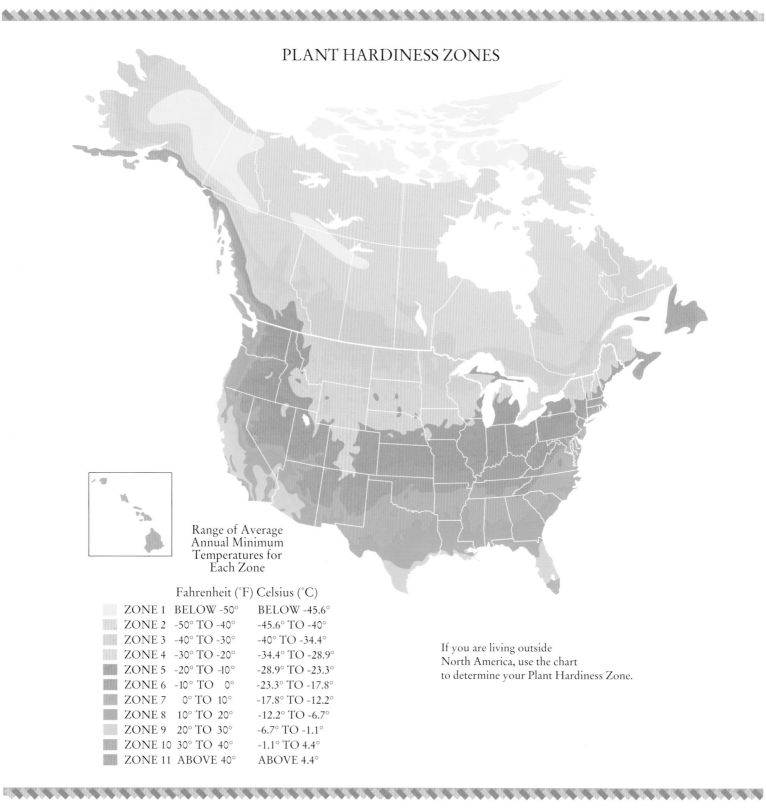

Range of Average
Annual Minimum
Temperatures for
Each Zone

		Fahrenheit (°F)	Celsius (°C)
	ZONE 1	BELOW -50°	BELOW -45.6°
	ZONE 2	-50° TO -40°	-45.6° TO -40°
	ZONE 3	-40° TO -30°	-40° TO -34.4°
	ZONE 4	-30° TO -20°	-34.4° TO -28.9°
	ZONE 5	-20° TO -10°	-28.9° TO -23.3°
	ZONE 6	-10° TO 0°	-23.3° TO -17.8°
	ZONE 7	0° TO 10°	-17.8° TO -12.2°
	ZONE 8	10° TO 20°	-12.2° TO -6.7°
	ZONE 9	20° TO 30°	-6.7° TO -1.1°
	ZONE 10	30° TO 40°	-1.1° TO 4.4°
	ZONE 11	ABOVE 40°	ABOVE 4.4°

If you are living outside
North America, use the chart
to determine your Plant Hardiness Zone.

GARDEN FEATURES

Anderson Design
P.O. Box 4057 C
Bellingham, WA 98227
800-947-7697
Arbors, trellises, gates, and
pyramids (Oriental, modern,
and traditional style)

Brooks Barrel Company
P.O. Box 1056
Department GD25
Cambridge, MD 21613-1046
410-228-0790
$2 for brochure
Natural-finish pine wooden
barrels and planters

Doner Design Inc.
Department G
2175 Beaver Valley Pike
New Providence, PA 17560
717-786-8891
Free brochure
Handcrafted landscape lights
(copper)

Kenneth Lynch & Sons
84 Danbury Road
P.O. Box 488
Wilton, CT 06897
203-762-8363
Free brochure
Benches, gates, scupture and stat-
uary, planters and urns, topiary,
sundials, and weathervanes

Kinsman Company
River Road
Department 351
Point Pleasant, PA 18950
800-733-4146
Free catalog
European plant supports, pillars,
arches trellises, flowerpots, and
planters

Lake Creek Garden Features Inc.
P.O. Box 118
Lake City, IA 51449
712-464-8924
Free brochure
Obelisks, plant stands, and gazing
globes and stands

Liteform Designs
P.O. Box 3316
Portland, OR 97208
503-253-1210
Garden lighting: path, bullard,
accent, step, and tree fixtures

New Blue Moon Studio
P.O. Box 579
Leavenworth, WA 98826
509-548-4754
Trellises, gates, arbors, and
garden furniture

Northwoods Nursery
27368 South Oglesby
Canby, OR 97013
503-266-5432
Free catalog and growing guide
Nursery features, ornamental
trees, shrubs, and vines

Stone Forest
Department G
P.O. Box 2840
Sante Fe, NM 87504
505-986-8883
Hand-carved granite birdbaths,
basins, fountains, lanterns, and
spheres

Valcovic Cornell Design
Box 380
Beverly, MA 01915
$4 for catalog, redeemable
with purchase
Trellises and arbor benches (tradi-
tional to contemporary style)

Wood Classics
Box 96G0410
Gardiner, NY 12525
914-255-5651
Free catalog
Garden benches, swings, chairs
and tables, rockers, lounges,
andumbrellas (all teak and
mahogany outdoor furniture)

PLANTS

Bear Creek Nursery
PO Box 411
Northport, WA 99157
Specializes in cold-hardy fruit
trees, shrubs, and berries

Busse Gardens
13579 10th St. NW
Cokato, MN 55321
612-286-2654
Fabulous hardy perennial plants

Comstock Seed
8520 W. 4th St.
Reno, NV 89523
702-746-3681
Seed supplier for drought-tolerant
native grasses and other plants of
the Great Basin

Forestfarm
990 Tetherow Road
Williams, OR 97544
503-846-7269
Catalog of more than two thou-
sand plants, including Western
natives, perennials, and an outstanding variety of trees and shrubs

The Fragrant Path
PO Box 328
Ft. Calhoun, NE 68023
Seeds for fragrant annuals, peren-
nials, shrubs, and vines, many of
them old-fashioned favorites

Gardens of the Blue Ridge
9056 Pittman Gap Road
P.O. Box 10
Pineola, NC 28662
Excellent selection of native trees
and shrubs

Goodwin Creek Gardens
P.O. Box 83
Williams, OR 97544
541-846-7375
Specializes in herbs, everlasting
flowers, and fragrant plants, as
well as plants that attract butter-
flies and hummingbirds

Holbrook Farm & Nursery
115 Lance Road
P.O. Box 368
Fletcher, NC 28732
Good selection of flowering shrubs

Jackson & Perkins
P.O. Box 1028
Medford, OR 97501
800-292-4769
Fine selection of roses, perennials,
and other garden-worthy plants

Kurt Bluemel, Inc.
2740 Green Lane
Baldwin, MD 31013
Excellent selection of ornamental
grasses, rushes, and sedges

Lilypons Water Gardens
PO Box 10
6800 Lilypons Road
Buckeystown, MD 21717
301-874-5133
Plants and supplies for water
gardens

Morden Nurseries, Ltd.
P.O. Box 1270
Morden, MB
Canada R0G 1J0
Wide selection of ornamental trees
and shrubs

Sources

Niche Gardens
1111 Dawson Rd.
Chapel Hill, NC 27516
919-967-0078
Good, healthy plants of grasses, nursery-propagated wildflowers, perennials, and herbs

Northwoods Nursery
27368 South Oglesby
Canby, OR 97013
503-266-5432
Ornamental trees, shrubs, and vines

Prairie Moon Nursery
Rt. 3 Box 163
Winona, MN 55987
507-452-1362
Generously sized plants and seeds of native prairie grasses and wildflowers

Prairie Nursery
P.O. Box 306
Westfield, WI 53964
608-296-3679
Catalog of prairie grasses and native wildflowers

Santa Barbara Heirloom Seedling Nursery
P.O. Box 4235
Santa Barbara, CA 93140
805-968-5444
Organically grown heirloom seedlings of vegetables, herbs, and edible flowers

Shady Oaks Nursery
112 10th Ave. SE
Waseca, MN 56093
507-835-5033
Specializes in plants that thrive in shade, including wildflowers, ferns, perennials, shrubs, and others

Shepherd's Garden Seeds
30 Irene Street
Torrington, CT 06790
860-482-0532
Fine selection of annuals, perennials, vegetables, and herbs

Southwestern Native Seeds
P.O. Box 50503
Tucson, AZ 85703
Responsibly collected wildflower seeds from the Southwest, West, and Mexico

Sunlight Gardens
Rt. 1 Box 600-A
Hillvale Rd.
Andersonville, TN 37705
615-494-8237
Wonderful selection of wildflowers, all nursery propagated

Tripple Brook Farm
37 Middle Rd.
Southampton, MA 01073
413-527-4626
Wildflowers and other Northeastern native plants, along with fruits and shrubs

Van Engelen Inc.
23 Tulip Drive
Bantam, CT 06750
Wide variety of bulbs

Van Ness Water Gardens
2460 N. Euclid Ave.
Upland, CA 91786
909-982-2425
Everything you could possibly need for a water garden, from plants to pools to supplies

Vermont Wildflower Farm
Rt. 7
Charlotte, VT 05445
802-425-3500
Excellent wildflower seed and seed mixes

Wayside Gardens
Garden Lande
Hodges, SC 29695
Offers a wide array of bulbs and perennials

We-Du Nurseries
Rt. 5 Box 724
Marion, NC 28752
704-738-8300
Incredible variety of wildflowers and native perennials from several continents, many woodland plants

Westgate Garden Nursery
751 Westgate Drive
Eureka, CA 95503
Large selection of rhododendrons and unusual ornamental shrubs and trees

White Flower Farm
P.O. Box 50
Litchfield, CT 06759
800-503-9624
Good selection of plants, including hostas, ferns, and hellebores

Wildlife Nurseries
P.O. Box 2724
Oshkosh, WI 54903
414-231-3780
Plants and seeds of native grasses, annuals, and perennials for wildlife; also water garden plants and supplies

Wildwood Gardens
14488 Rock Creek Road
Chardon, OH 44024
Collector's list of dwarf conifers and other dwarf shrubs

Woodlanders, Inc.
1128 Colleton Ave.
Aiken, SC 29801
803-648-7522
Excellent selection of native trees, shrubs, ferns, vines, and perennials, plus other good garden plants

Yucca Do Nursery
P.O. Box 655
Waller, TX 77484
409-826-6363
Good selection of trees, shrubs, and perennial plants, including many natives

CANADA

Corn Hill Nursery Ltd.
RR 5
Petitcodiac NB EOA 2HO

Ferncliff Gardens
SS 1
Mission, British Columbia
V2V 5V6

McFayden Seed Co. Ltd.
Box 1800
Brandon, Manitoba
R7A 6N4

Stirling Perennials
RR 1
Morpeth, Ontario
N0P 1X0

AUSTRALIA

Country Farm Perennials
RSD Laings Road
Nayook VIC 3821

Cox's Nursery
RMB 216 Oaks Road
Thrilmere NSW 2572

Honeysuckle Cottage Nursery
Lot 35 Bowen Mountain Road
Bowen Mountain via Grosevale
NSW 2753

Swan Bros Pty Ltd
490 Galston Road
Dural NSW 2158

Index

Abelia, 17, 50, 54, 85
Abies balsamea, 51
Acer, 20, 52, 87
Achillea filipendulina, 44
Achimenes, 85
Aconitum, 46
Actinidia, 97
Adiantum pedatum, 46
Agapanthus, 85
Ageratum, 77
Akebia, 95
Alchemilla, 47
Allamanda, 97
Allium, 51, 84
Aloysia triphylla, 51
Amelanchier alnifolia, 52
Anemone, 85
Anemopaegma, 96
Angelica archangelica, 51
Anthemis, 44, 51
Antirrhinum, 81
Arbors, 25, 89, 90, 94, 94
Arches, 90, 90, 94
Aristolochia, 97
Artemisia, 44, 51
Asarina, 95
Aster novae-belgii, 44
Astilbe, 46
Aubrieta, 82
Aucuba japonica, 47, 59
Aurinia, 82

Beaumontia, 97
Begonia, 46, 77, 82, 85
Berberis, 19, 20, 44, 47, 54, 85
Bergenia, 47
Boronia, 50
Bougainvillea, 77, 85
Brachycome iberidifolia, 50
Brick, 14, 26, 27, 27, 28
   clay, 27–28
   common, 28
   face, 28–29
   splits, 29
   used, 28
Browallia, 77, 81
Brugmansia candida, 50
Brunneria macrophylla, 46
Bryonopsis, 95
Buddleia, 44, 50, 50, 54
Buxus, 16, 54, 59, 85

Caladium, 85, 85
Calendula, 81
Calonyction, 97
Camellia, 46, 54, 86
Campanula, 44, 46, 82
Campsis, 95, 96
Canna, 85
Cardiospermum, 95
Carex elata, 46
Carissa macrocarpa, 19
Carpentaria californica, 50
Catharanthus, 77, 82
Celastrus, 95
Centaurea cyanus, 44
Cercidium floridum, 12
Cercis, 52, 53, 87
Cestrum nocturnum, 50
Chaenomeles, 54, 54
Chamaecyparis, 52, 86
Cheiranthus cheri, 50
Chimonanthus praecox, 50
Chiondoxa, 84
Citrus, 50, 87
Clarkia elegans, 44
Clematis, 50, 95
Clethra arborea, 46
Clivia, 85
Coleus, 77, 81
Container gardens, 56–87
Convolvulus cneorum, 44
Cornus, 46, 52, 52, 86, 87
Cotoneaster, 44, 47, 54
Courtyards
   enclosures, 15–19
   entrances, 8–21
   flooring, 13–14, 20, 20
   gardens, 12, 12
   planning, 19–20
Crataegus, 52, 87
Crinum, 85
Crocus, 84
Cryptomeria, 52
Cryptostegia, 97
Cumbalaria, 77
Cyclamen, 85, 85
Cytisus, 44, 50

Dahlia, 85
Daphne, 50, 54, 59–60
Deadheading, 70–71
Decumaria, 96
Deutzia scabra, 50

Dianthus, 44, 50, 81, 82
Dicentra spectabilis, 46
Dictamnus albus, 51
Digitalis, 47
Dining areas, 21, 21, 22, 23, 128–139
Dodecatheon pulchellum, 46
Dolichos, 97
Dryopteris filix-mas, 46

Eccremocarpus, 95
Elaeagnus pungens, 19, 86
Entrances, 8–21
Epimedium grandiflorum, 46
Eribotrya, 87
Escallonia rubra, 17
Eucomis, 85
Euonymus, 47, 86, 95, 96

Fatsia japonica, 47
Fences, 14, 14, 105, 105, 106, 106, 107, 107
Fertilizer, 48–49, 49
Ficus, 87, 95, 96
Flooring, 13–14, 20, 20
   aggregate, 29, 29, 30, 30
   bluestone, 27, 32, 32
   brick, 14, 26, 27–29
   concrete, 13, 26, 28, 29, 29, 30, 30, 31, 31, 33, 36, 37
   dressed stone, 35, 37
   fieldstone, 27, 35, 35
   flagstone, 13, 26, 27, 34, 34, 35, 37
   granite, 13, 14
   painting, 33–34
   patio, 26–39
   sealers, 13, 37
   slate, 13
   staining, 33–34
   tile, 13, 26, 37–39, 38, 39
Floriosa, 85
Forsythia, 86
Fountains, 11, 11, 118, 118, 119, 119
Freesia, 50, 85
Fuchsia, 46, 86

Galanthus, 84
Galtonia candicans, 50
Gardenia jasminoides, 50
Gaultheria procumbens, 46
Gazebos, 94
Gelsemium, 95
Gentiana asclepiadea, 46
Geranium, 44
Ginkgo, 87
Gladiolus, 85
Gleditsia triacanthos, 20
Gypsophila paniculata, 44

Halesia, 53, 53
Hedera, 46, 77, 95, 96
Hedges, 15, 16, 16, 17
Helianthemum, 44
Heliotropium, 50, 77
Helleborus, 46, 47
Hibbertia, 97
Hippeastrum, 85
Hosta, 46, 47
Houttuynia cordata, 46
Hoya carnosa, 50
Humulus, 97
Hyacinthus, 50, 84
Hydrangea, 46, 54, 54, 86, 95, 96
Hypericum, 44
Hyssopus officinalis, 51

Iberis, 77, 81, 82
Ilex, 19, 20, 54
Impatiens, 46, 77, 81, 82
Ipomoea, 97
Iris, 84
Irrigation
   automatic, 45
   drip, 64, 64, 65

Jasminum, 50, 95
Juniperus, 55, 86

Kalmia latifolia, 46
Kniphofia, 44

Lagerstroemia, 55, 55, 86
Lamium maculatum, 47
Lath houses, 91, 92, 92
Lathyrus, 50, 51, 59, 81
Laurus, 51, 87
Lavandula, 44, 50, 51, 86

Leucothoe fontanesiana, 46
Lighting, 100, 101, 102, 110, 110, 111, 111
   cross lighting, 112
   downlighting, 110, 110, 111
   installation, 112–115
   low-voltage, 113–115
   moonlighting, 111
   nightlighting, 100, 101
   uplighting, 111–112
Ligustrum, 16
Lilium, 50, 84, 84
Liriope muscari, 44
Lobelia, 77, 81
Lobularia, 77, 81
Lonicera, 95
Lupinus, 59
Lychnis chalcedonica, 44
Lycianthus, 97
Lysimachia, 82

Macfadyena, 96
Magnolia, 50, 53, 53, 87
Mahonia, 46, 55, 86
Malus, 53, 87
Mandevilla, 97
Meconopsis cambrica, 46
Menispermum, 97
Mentha suaveolens, 46
Michelia figo, 50
Monarda didyma, 51
Monstera, 96
Muscari, 50, 84
Myosotis odoratus, 59

Nandina, 86
Narcissus, 50, 84
Nemesia, 77, 81
Nepeta, 44
Nerium, 86
Nicotiana, 50, 82
Nierembergia, 82

Ocimum basilicum, 51
Origanum majorana, 51
Osmanthus, 47, 50, 86
Oxalis, 46, 85

Pachysandra terminalis, 47
Paeonia mlokosewitschii, 46
Papaver orientale, 44

Index

Parterres, 13
Parthenocissus, 95, 96
Patios, 22–39
    flooring, 26–39
    shapes, 24–25
    site analysis, 25–26
    sizes, 24–25
Pelargonium, 51, *51*, 77, 82
Pergolas, 25, 26, *88*, 89, 91, 92, *93*
Periploca, 97
Perovskia atriplicifolia, 44
Petunia, 50, 77, 81
Philadelphus coronarius, 50, *51*
Philodendron, 96
Phlox, 44, 50, 77
Photinia, 55, 86
Phyllostachys viridistriatus, 46
Picea, 53, 87
Pieris, 55, *55*, 86
Pinus, 59, 86
Pittosporum undulatum, 55
Planters, *40*, 41
    height, 44
    pockets, 45
    wells, 45, *45*
Planting, shrubs/trees, 65, 66, *66*, 68
Plants
    border, 49
    bulbs, 84–85
    container, 56–87
    dangerous, 18, 20, 109
    desert, 12
    for fragrance, 50–51
    hanging, 77
    perennial, 82
    screening, 103–104
    for shade, 46–47, 58
    succulents, 12
    for sun, 44, 58
    vines, 95–99
    water garden, 124–125
    winter care, 71, 7374
Play areas, 10
Plumaria rubra, 50
Podocarpus, 87
Polygonum, 46, 91, 95
Portulaca, 81
Posocarpus, 86

Potentilla fruticosa, 44
Primula, 77, 81, 82
Privacy, 10, 11, 100–115
Pruning, 68–71
Prunus, 16, *16*, 53, *53*, 87
Pulmonaria saccharata, 47
Pyracantha, 19, 20, 55, *55*
Pyrostegia, 96
Pyrus, 87

Ramadas, 91
Ranunculus, 85
Reseda odorata, 51
Rhododendron, 17, 46, 55
Rosa, *14*, 16, 17, 19, 51, 55, 86, 95
Rosmarinus officinalis, 44

Sagina, 77
Salvia, 81
Satureja, 51
Schindapsis, 96
Schizanthus, 81
Schizophragma, 95
Scilla, 84
Screens, 17, *17*, 18–19
Security, 11, 100–115
Shrubs
    deciduous, 19, 54, 55
    evergreen, 18, 54, 55
    thorny, 19
Skimmia japonica, 47
Smilacina racemosa, 46, 59
Soil, 47–49
    amendments, 60
    mixes, 60–63
    testing, 47, *48*
Solanum, 95
Sparaxis, 85
Spiraea, 55, 86
Stachys byzantina, 44
Sterbergia, 84
Stewartia pseudocamellia, 46
Styles
    formal, 12–13
    Native American, 12
    Oriental, 17, *17*
    Spanish, 11, *11*, *36*, *37*, *38*, 39
    traditional, 27
    Victorian, 27

Styrax japonicus, 53
Syringa, 51, 55, 86

Tagetes, 51, 77, 81
Taxus, 16, 19
Thalictrum aquilegifolium, 46
Thuja, 51, 53
Thunbergia, 95
Thymus, 51
Tigrida, 85
Trachelospermumn, 95
Tradescantia, 46
Trees
    for containers, 87
    deciduous, 18, 19, 52, 53, 59
    dwarf, 67, *67*
    evergreen, 18, 52, 53, 59
Trellises, 89, 91
Trillium grandiflorum, 46, 59
Trollius europaeus, 46
Tropaeolum, 47, 77, 82
Tulipa, 51, *51*, 84

Verbena, 77, 81
Viburnum, 51, 55, 86
Vinca minor, 47, 82
Vines
    for arbors, 98–99
    evergreen, 95
    perennial, 95
    for pergolas, 99
    for trellises, 99
    for walls and fences, 96–98
Viola, 44, 77, 81, 82

Walls, 11, *11*, 14, *14*, 15, *15*, 48, *48*
Water gardens, 116–127
Watering, 45, 64–65
Weigela, 55, 86
Wisteria, 51, 95

Yucca filamentosa, 44

Zantedeschia, 85
Zinnia, 82

GARDEN DESIGN CREDITS

Cover: *Rogers Gardens*
Page 10: *Lani Berrington & Associates*
Page 11, left: *Nick Williams & Associates*
Page 13: *Lani Berrington & Associates*
Page 15, left: *Rogers Gardens*
Page 15, right: *Susan Feller*
Page 17, left: *John Herbst, Jr. & Associates*
Page 17, right: *Rathfon Designs*
Page 20, right: *Erik Gronborg*
Page 21, left: *Nick Williams & Associates*
Page 21, right: *Jeff Stone Associates*
Page 24: *Nick Williams & Associates*
Page 25, right: *Ivy Reid*
Page 26: *Paradise Designs*
Page 27: *Gregg Bunch*
Page 28: *Bo Powell, Architect*
Page 29: *Environmental Creations, Inc.*
Page 30: *Charles E. Godfrey, Jr.*
Page 31: *Lani Berrington & Associates*
Page 32: *Design: Robert C. Chesnut, ASLA*
Page 34: *Rogers Gardens*
Page 36: *Environmental Creations, Inc.*
Page 38: *Charles E. Godfrey, Jr.*
Page 39: *Lani Berrington & Associates*

Pages 40–41: *Design: Blue Sky Designs*
Page 42: *Callaway Gardens*
Page 43: *Greg Grisamore & Associates*
Page 45: *Jim Whaley, Architect*
Page 48, right: *Rogers Gardens*
Pages 88–89: *Environmental Creations, Inc.*
Page 92: *Dennis Tromburg*
Page 93: *John Herbst, Jr. & Associates*
Page 94: *Ray Forsum, Landscape Architect*
Pages 100–101: *Blue Sky Designs*
Page 105, left: *Blue Sky Designs*
Page 107: *John Herbst, Jr. & Associates*
Page 108, left: *Rogers Gardens*
Page 111: *Night Shadows*
Page 112: *Night Shadows*
Page 114: *Sylvan Designs*
Page 118: *Rogers Gardens*
Page 126: *Lani Berrington & Associates*
Pages 128–129: *la STUDIO*
Page 132: *Nick Williams & Associates*
Page 134: *Rogers Gardens*
Page 136: *Environmental Creations, Inc.*
Page 137, left: *Rogers Gardens*
Page 137, right: *la STUDIO*
Page 138: *Environmental Creations, Inc.*

Photography ©Crandall and Crandall